SOUTHBANK

Nouvelle Vague

9 April – 31 May

Celebrating the 50th Anniversary
of French New Wave cinema including
François Truffaut's *Les Quatre cents coups*
and Jean-Luc Godard's *À bout de souffle*.

www.bfi.org.uk

Tickets 020 7928 3232
BFI Southbank London SE1 ⊖ Waterloo

Credit: À bout de souffle

GRANTA

12 Addison Avenue, London W11 4QR
email editorial@granta.com
To subscribe go to www.granta.com or call 020 8955 7011

ISSUE 105

This selection copyright © 2009 Granta Publications.
In the United States, *Granta* is published in association with Grove/Atlantic Inc,
841 Broadway, 4th Floor, New York, NY 10003, and distributed by PGW.

Granta is printed and bound in Italy by Legoprint.
This magazine has been printed on paper that has been certified by the Forest Stewardship Council (FSC).

ISBN 978-1-905881-05-5

International PEN presents

A Celebration of World Literature
16 - 19 April 2009

Returning for its second year this spring, Free the Word! takes the theme Heaven and Earth, as the great writers you know and the great writers you don't explore beyond the imagination and through other worlds in an explosive weekend of storytelling, discussion and debate.

Nadine Gordimer (South Africa)
Azar Nafisi (Iran)
Lee Stringer (USA)
Lydia Cacho (Mexico)
Florian Zeller (France)
Leila Aboulela (Sudan)
Jack Mapanje (Malawi/UK)
Christian Jungersen (Denmark)
Carolin Emcke (Germany)
Catherine Millet (France)
Samir El-youssef (Lebanon/UK)

and many more ...

Events take place at Shakespeare's Globe, Southwark Playhouse and the Young Vic

To book and for more information on all Free the Word! events visit www.internationalpen.org.uk

Sponsored by

Bloomberg

LOTTERY FUNDED

CONTENTS

Five Spice Street

Can Xue Translated by Karen Gernant and Chen Zeping

Chinese author Can Xue's *Five Spice Street* stands out as one of the most astonishing novels written in any language over the last twenty years.
The first of Xue's full-length works to be translated into English, this compelling book explores a secret that takes on a life of its own as neighbours speculate, argue, indulge their fantasies and reveal their deepest anxieties.
352pp. £14.99

Songbook

The Selected Poems of Umberto Saba
Umberto Saba

Translated by George Hochfield and Leonard Nathan
Introduction, Notes and Commentary by George Hochfield

Umberto Saba is regarded as one of the most important Italian poets of the early twentieth century. This bilingual volume at last brings an extensive and exquisitely translated collection of Saba's poems to English-speaking readers.
592pp. £20.00

SONGBOOK THE SELECTED POEMS OF UMBERTO SABA

One State, Two States

Resolving the Israel/Palestine Conflict
Benny Morris

Tackling one of the world's most perplexing and divisive issues, renowned historian Benny Morris considers the legacy of the 1948 Arab-Israeli war, previous proposed solutions to the conflict between Palestinians and Israel, and the viability of various options for the future.
Available May 256pp. 7 b/w maps £18.99

BENNY MORRIS
ONE STATE, TWO STATES
RESOLVING THE ISRAEL/PALESTINE CONFLICT

My Happiness Bears No Relation to Happiness

A Poet's Life in the Palestinian Century
Adina Hoffman

This beautifully written biography of the internationally renowned Palestinian poet Taha offers a compelling portrait of the man as well as a nuanced, deeply human view of the tragedy of the Israeli-Palestinian conflict. Taha's story, like his poetry, is at once profoundly local and utterly universal.
Available May 464pp. 65 b/w illus. £17.99

My Happiness Bears No Relation to Happiness
A Poet's Life in the Palestinian Century

yale *www.yalebooks.co.uk*

The vanishing point

When something is lost, our first instinct is often towards preservation: either of the thing itself, its memory and its traces in the world, or of the part of us that is affected by what is now missing. The pieces in this issue of *Granta* reflect on the complex business of salvage and try to bring into the light what we discover when we come face to face with loss.

It is rarely a straightforward process. Jeremy Treglown's thought-provoking exploration of the gathering movement to exhume the victims of the Spanish Civil War amply demonstrates the tensions created when a desire to commemorate clashes with a desire to move forward, and when both entirely natural impulses are claimed by other agendas. Although his investigation illuminates the continuing aftermath of a particularly dark and disastrous episode in Spanish history, it has clear parallels with other countries' attempts to recover from traumatic events and forces us to question whether an apparently simple urge to remember and to pay tribute can remain uninflected by other equally complex concerns.

A similar ambiguity informs Maurice Walsh's dispatch from Ireland, where he travelled to spend time with the Catholic priests whose numbers have been diminishing over the past few decades. He reports of a decline in vocations that coincided with a widespread rise in secularism and an attitude towards the Church that hardened – perhaps irreversibly – after the wave of child-abuse scandals in the 1990s, which were seen not merely as instances of individual wrongdoing but as evidence of a collusion between a powerful

Move on with Arvon.
Creative writing
in historic houses.
Grants available.

Visit www.arvonfoundation.org

hierarchy and those whom it had sent into the community as trusted individuals. This shift in perspective has been well documented and, when the writer and I spoke about the piece in its earliest stages, we agreed that a fruitful focus would be what the priests themselves felt about this process of marginalization.

Elsewhere, we feature some extremely personal stories, perhaps none more so than Melanie McFadyean's 'Missing', which relates the experiences, over nearly two decades, of the Needham family. Ben Needham, a child of twenty-one months, disappeared on the Greek island of Kos in 1991; he has never been found. The moment of his disappearance – the moment when he was last seen by members of his family – resonates through her account with its utter simplicity; a child, playing in the sun, running in and out of doors, being completely childlike and completely unselfconscious. Then silence, and absence; and then the continuing lives of Ben's mother, Kerry, his grandparents, his uncles and the sister born after he disappeared. It is a familiar fictional device, and often characteristic of the stories we tell ourselves about defining periods in our lives, to suggest that everything can change in an instant. Much of the time, that is not really true, and rather more likely that a crisply delineated sequence of events allows us to cope with chaos and confusion. In the case of the Needhams, though, even that world-altering single moment, viewed through the prism of different people and the passage of time, can remain painfully resistant to closure.

There is a different kind of examination of the past going on in Elizabeth Pisani's 'Chinese Whispers', in which the author recalls the night that she spent in Tiananmen Square twenty years ago, frantically attempting to phone in reports to her news agency as tanks (not to be confused with armoured personnel carriers, as her bosses on the other end of the line curtly impressed on her) rolled in to crush the ranks of pro-democracy protestors filling the Square.

But Pisani's resurrection of a night that, to her, an inexperienced reporter of twenty-four, was the most momentous she had ever lived through, proves rather harder to pin down in the retelling. Is her version of events correct to the last detail? Or has she embroidered and finessed her memories in the intervening years?

Sometimes, of course, the changing of the guard makes room for us to cast a lighter eye over events, as in Don Paterson's piece of memoir, which tells of his youthful passion – and passion *is* the right word – for evangelical Christianity, an effort to exoticize his everyday life that led to fervent prayer sessions enlivened by the odd bout of angeloglossia. It seems that what he discovered as his faith faded was an unshakeable enthusiasm for rational thought. But he also conjures, as the best memoirs do, a portrait of another time – in this case, a world of weak tea, Jammie Dodgers and fearsome bullies. Equally evocative are the pipe smokers, captured in Andrew Martin's ode to a pleasure in peril, who have found themselves defending their commitment to a slower, temptingly detached way of life – their special brand of 'hypnotic latency', as Martin puts it.

In among these surveys of vanishing worlds come three pieces of fiction: an artfully poignant story by Janet Frame, a wry tale of dentistry and disarray by A. L. Kennedy and two pieces of work by Altán Walker. *Of Earthly Love*, Walker's debut novel, was several years in the writing, rewriting and recasting and had yet to be finished when the writer died in 2007. As I began to read the manuscript, knowing that it would never now be completed, I felt immediately that if it were to remain unseen readers would be deprived of a true delight; one that would introduce them to a wild, shifting, ungovernable voice, capable of great acts of ventriloquism and imagination. It is a real pleasure to be able to publish part of Walker's manuscript here and to know that, in among the varieties of loss that we are often subject to, there remain treasures to find. ■

Documentary

I keep imagining another place:

somewhere from one of those slightly too plausible films
where the street is a parallel street in a parallel world

and everything altered slightly, though not that much,
only another version of what we know

going about its business, our parallel selves
brighter and more successful than we seem,

but touched, still, with a possibility:
the parallel, we're led to guess,

of *us*.
        So it continues, one world feeding the next
with minor variations, like the days

we pass so calmly, unaware of all this
business: quarks

and singularities,
and everything coming to light in a fold of time

where something that never was, or might have been,
occurs, at last, in some infinity,

to people much like us, though not quite us,
who think of us more fondly than we know.

A top-sail schooner of the mind

From my upstairs windows in Llanystumdwy, near Cricieth in Gwynedd, I can look out on Cardigan Bay, and the sea runs through our house – not literally, of course, but metaphorically, or perhaps emotionally.

The house is infested with ship models old and new – sailing ships, plastic French trawlers, fishing craft from Greece, Venice and Sri Lanka, a New York tug, a Hong Kong ferry, a tall-funnelled steamer from old Danzig, an ancient Hong Kong junk appositely named *Fair Wind, Great Profit*. Of all this motley fleet, the undoubted flagship is the three-masted top-sail schooner *Owen Morris*, because so much sentiment is invested in her.

There is a touch of pathos, for a start. The model was built for me by the late Mr Bertie Japheth, who came from a seafaring family of Trefor, a few miles from here, but who could not himself go to sea because of physical disability. In recompense he devoted himself to the meticulous making of models, and so the *Owen Morris* carries for me a cargo of affectionate and admiring regret.

Then there is patriotic pride. The model is so totally Welsh, and so totally local an artefact. The ship itself carried my family name of course, a name very common in these parts. She was built, in 1891, just along the coast at Porthmadog. She was jointly owned by several citizens of that town, including the eponymous Owen and two other Morrises, and her crew of six were all local men. Everyone knew everyone else in the small Welsh sea towns of those days, and when I look out from my window at the now silent and empty sea, I feel I can still see her sailing by, waved on her way by friends and relatives, deep-loaded with slate from the Snowdon mountains, manned by cousins, uncles and schoolmates.

She was so small a ship – only 167 tons – and yet so proud, so heroic of meaning, and it tugs at my heart to see her in fancy out at sea, in wood and copper miniature at home. She was only one of the many little schooners which once sailed from Porthmadog past my house to the far reaches of the oceans – Welsh-built ships, Welsh-owned ships, Welsh-speaking ships, in the days long gone when so much of Wales was, at least in romantic fancy, a kind of family.

I don't suppose there is another model of her anywhere, so in a way I am the final Morris owner of the schooner *Owen Morris*, and besides those feelings of pride and sympathy that she conveys, as it happens she carries too an echo of another sea that has meant much to me. Years ago I noticed that in a rather obscure painting by Vittore Carpaccio, above a cavalcade of holy persons in some ceremonial chamber, a model of a Venetian galleon was mounted on a beam – not suspended from it, but standing grandly on top. In emulation that's how my *Owen Morris* stands today, and among the lesser models of her command, up there on subsidiary beams, there sail in tribute two red-sailed fishing craft direct from that other haven of my emotions, the Venetian lagoon.

In the end epic attended my little ship of ships. On December 9, 1907 she sailed past my house on the very last lap of a long voyage home. She had taken slates to Hamburg, then sailed on to Newfoundland with a cargo of salt, back across the Atlantic with salt cod for Genoa, finally scudding homeward through rough seas in ballast towards Porthmadog. Almost within sight of my window a squall ran her aground on the promontory called Craig Ddu, Black Rock, only a mile or two from harbour.

The Cricieth lifeboat was alerted, and hundreds of people

crowded to the shore to help with its launch – after chapel, for it was a Sunday morning. The *Owen Morris* was fast breaking up in a raging sea. Greatly daring the lifeboat pulled alongside, under a reefed lugsail, and in brief moments of contact all the crew leaped to safety. Within minutes the remains of the shattered vessel were swept into a cave in the flank of the promontory, and the ship's bell, so eyewitnesses said, was left tolling there 'in melancholy notes'.

I hear it tolling still, when I am in the mood, but I am happy to think that all the crew of the *Owen Morris* were saved in such a neighbourly way, and touched to know that to this day one last timber of the real *Owen Morris* hangs on a wall of the Prince of Wales pub down the road in Cricieth. Her loss cost the Portmadog Mutual Insurance Company £1,600, but her reincarnation earned dear Bertie Japheth a bob or two, and I have to admit that all in all her replica does stand there rather smugly on its beam of Welsh oak. ■

Mass graves in the San Rafael cemetery, Málaga, December 2008

THE MEMORY MOVEMENT

Decades after the end of the Spanish Civil War,
its victims are at the heart of a fiercely contested battle

Jeremy Treglown

Ignacio Ruíz Vara is a security guard in Málaga. He grew up there, as did his father and grandfather. There's plenty of work these days for people in his business, especially looking after second homes and holiday developments, augmented now by building projects abandoned 'until the economy picks up'. His own duties changed, though, two years ago, when he volunteered to take charge of the cemetery of San Rafael, a sixteen-acre sprawl on the west side of the town. This was originally the place where Málaga's poor, *los humildes*, were buried. It was well outside the old town, in the middle of farmland mainly given over to sweet potatoes. Now the area – on the way to the huge tourist airport – is part industrial, part social housing. There was once a small chapel here with a lamp outside, but it was demolished to make way for a wider road. Much of the original cemetery wall has fallen down too and been replaced with high temporary fencing. A single-storey gatehouse still stands and this is where the guard has his base. The cemetery gates are kept locked.

The reason Ignacio volunteered, and the reason the cemetery has a security guard in the first place, is that among its dead are at least 4,000 people – mostly men but also women and children – who were executed without trial between 1936 and 1955: the period of Spain's civil war and of the long, grim first phase of Francisco Franco's dictatorship. Almost all are in *fosas comunes*, mass graves.

Suddenly, the whole of Spain seems to be searching for its disappeared. They are everywhere – in every region, in every kind of terrain. Families who have stayed silent for decades are being urged, very often by the victims' grandchildren, to say what they suspect, or know, or saw. Even the government is encouraging them. Under the Law of Historical Memory passed in October, 2007, anyone who can produce reasonable evidence of the existence of a mass grave is entitled to help in excavating it. The dotted map of likely sites, between the Basque country and Andalucía, Castilla-León and Valencia, makes the peninsula look like the face of a child with chickenpox.

Even as far as Málaga alone is concerned, no one knows how long the job will take, or how many *fosas* – let alone skeletons – are still to be found there. It's being done very systematically, under the directorship of a senior archaeologist, Sebastián Fernández. The project – locally based but loosely connected to a national programme – is paid for jointly by the town, the province of Andalucía and the University of Málaga, where Fernández heads the humanities faculty. As each grave is opened, the contents are cleaned, measured, photographed, put into separate boxes and kept for DNA testing. Once all the exhumations are finished, the whole area will be turned into a park. In the middle will be a memorial carrying the names of everyone who can possibly be named.

One of the skeletons at Málaga belongs to Ignacio's paternal grandfather, Diego Ruíz Schacht, though Ignacio doesn't know whether it's among those that have already been dug up. He says he isn't superstitious; he doesn't imagine that Diego's spirit haunts the place, or is anywhere, in fact, but he is proud of his grandfather and shows me the picture he carries in his wallet. Diego was a pro-democracy member of the Guardia Civil, well known, Ignacio says, for his resistance to corruption. Like other republicans in the police, he was picked off for elimination early in the Civil War.

By the time of Diego's death, the family had already seen a lot of changes. The military dictatorship which had taken over Spain in 1923 collapsed seven years later and the king abdicated. In 1931 an elected democratic government was installed – Spain's first ever. It commanded the loyalty of working people and liberal intellectuals, but was weakened by internal divisions, by the apparent impossibility of solving the country's economic difficulties, and by left-wing extremism of a kind which gave encouragement to its equivalent on the right. The Falange – Spain's fascist party – was founded soon after. In July 1936, Francisco Franco, a career soldier who had come to prominence in the army's struggle to hang on to 'Spanish' Morocco, led a kind of colonial invasion in reverse, against the home country. He had the support of most of Spain's disproportionately large number of army officers, most of the middle and upper classes and almost all of the still-powerful bishops. While Britain and France prevaricated over whether or not to back Spain's elected government, the coup gained immediate aid – including troops and weapons – from Hitler and Mussolini. Often called the Second World War's dress rehearsal, the Spanish Civil War is better seen as its first act.

Franco's own soldiers were a mix of hardened Spanish legionaries and North African mercenaries, and in the Málaga region they were quickly reinforced not only by rebel troops based on the mainland but by fascist Italian motorized columns with light tanks. The port was bombed from the air, shelled from the sea, then invaded by land. The slaughter of fleeing civilians horrified even hardened observers, the writers Arthur Koestler and Franz Borkenau among them. Afterwards, the rebels undertook a long purge of key republican sympathizers, which continued into the 1940s under the notorious local prosecutor Carlos Arias Navarro, 'the Butcher of Málaga'. Diego's turn came in March 1937, when he was picked up at home in the middle of town.

The scene was often described to the young Ignacio by his

grandmother, who lived to be ninety-nine, and also by a friend's father who was in the same Guardia company as Diego. It's generally said that victims were shot against the cemetery wall, by the light from the chapel. Ignacio takes a practical view: 'The place is very big. It's a long way to carry a lot of dead bodies. I think they were mostly shot inside, beside the graves.'

Salud Alberto Zarzuela, Catalina Alcaraz, Cristina Carillo Franco, Teresa Castro Ramírez, Ana Fernández Ramírez, Isabel Gómez, her sister Josefa Gómez and their niece Lolita Gómez, Teresa Menacho, María Nogales Castro, Antonia Pérez Vega, Maria Rincón Barea and her sister Jerónima Rincón Barea, Isabel Román Montes, Natividad Vilchez.

These are the names of fifteen women in their twenties whose remains – along with those of a teenaged boy who, it's said locally, was forced to dig the grave – were found last summer among the cork oak plantations of Grazalema, a much-visited beauty spot in the mountains west of Ronda. They hadn't been involved in politics, unless you count the possibility that one of them may have been engaged to a republican. Four were heavily pregnant. How they died hasn't yet been established. No bullets were found. If stories about other atrocities in the region are anything to go by, the women were probably raped, tortured and then buried alive – those, that is, who survived that long. In many such cases, reprisals were the main motive: men loyal to the republican government waged a particularly effective guerrilla campaign against rebel forces in the area.

Another common purpose of capturing women was to use them as hostages, in the hope of inducing republicans who had gone into hiding to surrender. Whether or not this worked, other impulses often took over. But 'nationalism' – as Franco's movement called itself, to the fury of patriots on the other side – was intrinsically brutal, closely linked as it was to fascism, founded on decades of imperial skirmishing in Morocco and, before that, on notions of racial and ideological purification – *limpieza* – that went back via the Inquisition to Spain's earliest expulsions of Muslims and Jews.

Spanish historians have recently shown that some supporters of Franco regarded socialism as a hereditary form of biological degeneracy. On this basis, it's argued that the rebels' avowed aim to exterminate the enemy, including women and children, was tantamount to genocide. Generals tend, of course, to threaten to wipe out the other side – it's a good way of persuading people to surrender – but you don't have to accept the genocide theory to be able to imagine the effect of the nightly radio broadcasts put out by the main rebel propagandist, General González Queipo de Llano, on impressionable, armed young men. Queipo's threats against his enemy gave substance to the nihilistic gibberish of Falangism, with its war cry '*Viva la muerte!*' ('Long live death'.)

'Even if they're already dead, I shall kill them again,' Queipo famously roared, and – in a phrase that to some survivors gives an unwelcome, if fortuitous, colouring to present events – 'Even if they hide beneath the earth, I shall dig them out.' Queipo urged his troops to rape republican women and added to the stimulus by telling stories of sado-sexual feats already performed by their fellows in arms. YOUR WOMEN WILL GIVE BIRTH TO FASCISTS was a common piece of graffiti in recently conquered republican towns and villages.

There are places where the executioners' work appears to have been more calmly organized. In the grave I watched being excavated in Málaga, most of the skeletons lie straight, close together, side by side or head to toe, many with their hands tied. In this particular spot there are, one of the diggers cheerfully explained to me, '*tres plantas*', three storeys. We were standing on the top floor, but pushing up from the level below were the dome of a forehead, a knee. You had to tread carefully.

Even here, though, the neat rows are occasionally interrupted by signs of anger, exasperation, revenge: bodies at an angle, arms thrown above the head, a pelvis with a bullet lodged in the groin. Elsewhere, we can be sure that how people died often involved the worst they could have feared. Federico García Lorca, the dramatist and poet, is such a case.

E xuberant, handsome, spoiled, uncontrollable, extravagantly gifted, Lorca always dreaded death. He used his feelings about it, as well as about sex – his homosexuality, his mix of fascination with and horror of female sexuality – in his work. Like the film-maker Pedro Almodóvar today, he was as well known abroad as he was in Spain, with the result that the hostility of Spaniards who disliked his art, or just the idea of it, was compounded by a sense that they themselves were being impugned by it – that he gave Spain a bad name. But to think about the Civil War in these international terms runs the risk of forgetting its intense localization. In regions such as Lorca's native Granada, participants often had relatives on both sides; they had gone to church and to school together, had friends and enemies in common, knew each other's secrets, fantasies and jealousies. When Lorca became famous outside Granada, some of those left behind were possessively, competitively proud, while others were envious. He was close to Salvador Dalí, to Luis Buñuel, names with highly charged associations of their own.

Among the most vocal supporters of the current wave of exhumations is Lorca's biographer Ian Gibson, whose first book, published – though not in Spain – when Franco was still in power, is an account of the poet's murder. Irish by birth, Gibson has taken Spanish nationality and lives in Madrid, where people in the street and in bars come up to shake his hand. His measured, perfectly judged description of the poet's last days relates the intricacies of regional politics in the Granada of July and August 1936, especially in the Falange and the military garrison: the publicity given in local papers to the poet's return to what he hoped was the safety of his parents' home; the petty but genuine anger he had recently caused with a published attack on the middle class; the family's mounting apprehension when their house was searched; its first wartime bereavement, when Lorca's brother-in-law, the socialist mayor of Granada, was shot; Lorca's sheer panic; the shelter bravely given him by family friends who belonged to the Falange. Crucial in all this is a psychological drama in which the main protagonist other than Lorca

Federico García Lorca *c.*1936. Spanish writer, poet and dramatist: 1898–1936

himself was an ambitious, pompous and, of late, much derided and humiliated conservative, Ramón Ruíz Alonso, who had been in and out of the Spanish parliament as a representative of Granada. The military rebellion brought him the first real power he knew how to use and he nursed a personal hatred of 'the poet with the big fat head' and everything he represented. On the afternoon of August 16, 1936 Alonso and two other extremely unpleasant men came to get him.

Accounts of what happened next differ and it is the mixture of uncertainty and the raw facts we have that makes the story so powerful. We know that Lorca was imprisoned for at least two days and that he was unable to conceal his terror. We can guess that this of itself gave encouragement as well as scope to his tormentors. We know that, handcuffed to a republican schoolmaster, Dióscoro Galindo González, he was taken to Víznar, in the hills behind Granada, then a rebel fortification and a place of execution where, night after night, consignments of prisoners were handed over to the 'Black Squad': men who had volunteered for this work because they enjoyed it. They were killed and buried with two other prisoners. The following morning, one of the party that originally arrested the poet, a landowning playboy friend of Alonso, was heard boasting that he had just helped to shoot Lorca and had fired 'two bullets into his arse for being queer'.

So much for what's known. What isn't known for certain is where the bodies were buried. Today, there are two monuments to Lorca. One is in a dip in what's now a wooded park above Víznar, close to a footpath which runs around the hillside, past what you would never know is a vast mass grave – the trees were originally planted soon after the war to help conceal it – to the next village, Alfáca. The other is at the end of this path, behind a padlocked gate. A great deal of debate has been given to the question of which place, if either, contains Lorca's remains and, in the current climate, there is strong pressure towards digging up both sites. The obvious questions, in Lorca's case and more generally, are: why, and then what?

Until recently, the poet's nephews and nieces have been united, at least in public, in arguing that the best way to remain true to Spain's history is to leave the dead where they are. As the campaign in favour of exhumations has gained momentum, though, descendants of the men with whom Lorca was buried have decided that they would like the bodies to be exhumed and this has forced the family to reconsider. Even archaeologists, after all, can't excavate a *fosa común* selectively. Practicalities apart, the case has helped bring into focus some wider complications in the current debates about memory.

In the first place, Spanish attitudes to the dead have always included an apparently paradoxical mix of reverence and casualness. Graves are visited with a degree of ceremony on the Feast of All Souls, every November – the opening sequence of Almodóvar's *Volver*, in which Penélope Cruz and her friends squeakily polish rows of tombstones, is funny because it satirizes a recognizable fact of life. But because of the rockiness of much southern European ground, many graves here are not holes in the ground but concrete storage blocks full of human-sized pigeonholes: slots in a wall into which each coffin slides neatly, followed by a slab of stone, cemented in. Tombs of this kind are leased, not owned. The initial payment lasts for a fixed period, but if no more rent is forthcoming after that, the corpse is evicted to a charnel house in the cemetery corner. Visitors carrying their respectful bunches of flowers or plastic wreaths can be all too conscious of an untidy pile of bones and rotting hair close by. The relics of saints, whether religious or secular, involve similar contradictions. Few people among the crush of pilgrims at Santiago de Compostela can be unaware that the widely distributed bones attributed to the patron saint are far too many to have come from one skeleton. As for Christopher Columbus, it's thought that his son Diego's remains may at some point have been mistaken for his in the course of a series of moves in which father or son or both were successively interred, dug up and reburied in Spain, Hispaniola, Cuba and then back in Seville.

In this context, the fact that so many Civil War graves were left unmarked itself raises questions. While it was dangerous to pay overt attention to a republican grave during the Civil War and the repressive years after it, there must have been opportunities to leave a few stones as indicators. Could it be that at least some of those immediately concerned – especially the more rationalist, secular republicans – didn't think the exact whereabouts of the dead all that important? The novelist Javier Marías feels so. One of his uncles was killed in Madrid, together with a group of fellow students. According to Marías, his mother and her siblings were too busy surviving to go in search of his body and, later, the family simply felt that his remains – wherever they were – were best left with those of his friends.

There are also arguments about the way that – as in many other parts of the world – 'memory' seems to have become a tool of party politics and personal advancement. Among the most discussed examples are recent interventions by Judge Baltasar Garzón, best known in the anglophone world for his 1998 attempt, making unprecedented use of 'universal jurisdiction', to get General Pinochet of Chile extradited to Spain on a charge of crimes against humanity. That move helped awaken interest in past atrocities in Garzón's home country, akin to those for which Pinochet was arraigned. Last summer, Garzón belatedly threw his weight behind the exhumations campaign by reminding various laggardly authorities of their obligations under the 2007 Law of Historical Memory, which, among other things, requires them to assist excavations and archival searches and – except in cases of special architectural or historical merit – to remove memorials to Franco's dictatorship.

Some of his demands seemed quixotic, not to say dictatorial. Acting on behalf of a number of families, he announced, for example, that he needed complete lists of the names of Civil War casualties within two weeks. While historians of the twentieth century were delighted to see archivists being put under pressure to make documentary records more readily available, they also pointed out that the quantity of material is vast. A comparable investigation of records of the Nazi concentration camp at Mauthausen, where many thousands of Spanish republicans who had fled north were imprisoned and died, took eight years to establish the identities of some 4,000 prisoners and is still far from complete. It isn't difficult to calculate from this the time that would be involved in supplying a reasonably accurate list of – say – the 20,000 or so people murdered in Spain just in the summer of 1936. A full census of Civil War dead would involve seven or eight times that number.

Legal opponents of Garzón have successfully argued that the 2007 memory law leaves responsibility with local rather than central authorities (democratic Spain is highly devolved, administratively) and that he has been exceeding his powers. But he has never held back from the big gesture. He has demanded, for example, that any surviving senior officials of the Franco regime should be prosecuted for crimes against humanity. Reminded of the amnesty passed by the elected Spanish government in 1977, he replied that no amnesty can trump human rights. Meanwhile, he continues to press for action on the findings of historians who have shown both that Francoist military psychologists experimented on republican prisoners in the hope of identifying 'red genes' and that thousands of young children of republican women, including ones born in prison, were handed over to Francoist couples or to religious orders and given new identities. Many of these forced adoptees are still alive and some have recently found out who their real parents were.

Law is a blunter instrument than history. Garzón's advocacy, which includes among its causes the opening of Lorca's grave, can seem shrill by comparison with the patient work he draws on. As one of Lorca's nephews has complained, 'We don't need a judge to come and tell us Franco was a murderer.' In his late thirties, Garzón was closely associated with the left-of-centre PSOE (Partido Socialista Obrero Español – Spanish Socialist Workers' Party) and was briefly in charge of its anti-drug campaign. After returning to power in 2004, the PSOE under José Luis Rodríguez Zapatero immediately began pushing through its Law of Historical Memory, with the probably intentional effect of inducing key members of the conservative Partido Popular to oppose it. By walking into this trap, the current leader of the PP, Mariano Rajoy, has allowed his party to be seen as not only the defender but the natural heir of Francoism – and the PSOE, by contrast, as an idealized version of the republican movement made new. (Zapatero himself speaks often about one of his grandfathers, who was killed by the Francoists, but not about the other, who was on their side.) No one, meanwhile, accuses Baltasar Garzón of crude partisanship; he has been an implacable rooter-out of corruption in the PSOE, as in other quarters. But by turning himself into a popular hero of the memory movement, he can't have harmed his chances if he should choose to return to politics.

Yet another source of disagreement – perhaps the most emotionally powerful – derives from a generation gap. To be sure, some of the first proponents of the exhumations were survivors of the Civil War. In Málaga, I met a locally revered man named Francisco Espinosa, born in 1931, whose father, one of the Falange's victims, is buried in the cemetery of San Rafael. Espinosa began an association '*contra el olvido*' ('against amnesia') in Málaga as early as 1977. Several other people who remember the dictatorship, though, expressed doubts to me: doubts that often seemed to contain an element of injured pride. The peaceful transition to democracy, in their eyes, was a triumph. Anyone over fifty not only lived through it but played their part. To be told now, by people the same ages as their own children, that they had paid insufficient respect to the past was hard to take. The pragmatic *pacto de olvido* (agreement to forget, or overlook) of the early post-Franco period may be derided today, but it served a crucial purpose.

So far as it existed, that is. In *El País* last September, the novelist and columnist Antonio Muñoz Molina attacked the memory movement, arguing that its proponents are merely indulging themselves with the fantasy that, without having to make much effort or put themselves in any danger, they are somehow rectifying a major historical injustice:

> The result of this sentimentalization and officialization of memory
> is itself a form of amnesia... Anyone who claims that only now is it
> possible to publish novels or history books which tell the truth about
> the Civil War and the dictatorship would do better to say that he or

she has not read the ones that were written earlier, or can't be
bothered to read them because they are unfashionable.

I met the writer in Madrid and he expanded on his theme with
good-humoured exasperation. 'You see pictures in the newspapers and
on television of people too young to have any memory of the Civil
War, in tears because some skeletons have their hands tied. *Of course*
their hands were tied!'

All these criticisms have good sense behind them. To a detached
outsider there *is* something futile about going in search of bodies
buried seventy-odd years ago. It *is* a pity that sentiment about a distant
war is being exploited for current political ends. The older generation
does, by and large, have a juster, more complex understanding of the
mid-twentieth century than do younger people. As I was told by a
recently retired bystander at a new exhumation, 'There are more than
two sides to these questions.' He pointed out that no one seems
bothered about the remaining mass graves of 'nationalists'. And there
are still other arguments to be heard, particularly that the memory
vogue is being exaggerated by the media, that it is in danger of opening
old wounds and that it distracts attention from more urgent problems
such as the environment and the economy. Spain, after all, now has to
deal with one of the steepest increases in unemployment in Europe.

Lorca, meanwhile, as many have pointed out, survives in his works;
finding his bones won't make any difference. Most of the dead, though,
have no special claim on historical memory and it may be the very fact
that survivors of the Civil War are fast dying off that makes a younger
generation so eager to learn about their family's experiences at that
time and to commemorate those who were killed. The humbler they
were, in fact, and the more meaningless their deaths, the stronger this
impulse can be.

Marina Gómez Pastor lives with her parents and sister in
Valdecaballeros, a small town remote even by the standards of
its region, Extremadura, in Spain's south-west. She is the eldest

A still from Luis Buñuel's film *Tierra sin pan*, also known as *Land without Bread*, *Las Hurdes* and *Unpromised Land*, 1932

granddaughter of Benilde Ruíz Fernández, a widow who was a permanent presence in her life as she was growing up in the 1980s and 90s. This was the period Spaniards call 'the Transition': the initially precarious shift to democracy after Franco's death in 1975. By general – though far from unanimous – consent, it seemed best then not to talk too much about the past, or not publicly. Who knew how long the new regime would last? A constitution took three years to draft. During this time, Spain was at first ruled by governments appointed by the young and as yet untested King Juan Carlos – the first of them led by none other than the former Butcher of Málaga, Carlos Arias Navarro. Most of the structures Franco had set up remained in place and the army was loyal to his memory. Organized democratic political parties and trade unions were slow to gain strength, the Basque separatist group ETA was very active and, when a general election was eventually held in 1977, it left in power Adolfo Suárez – an adroit, liberal centrist but, again, one who had begun his political career under Franco. Three years later, there was a serious attempt at another military coup.

Besides, during the dictatorship, with its censors, its propaganda, its high-handed policing and its mysterious disappearances, people had almost forgotten what it meant to talk openly about anything that mattered. Conversation was less restricted, though, *en casa*, and as time passed and the new freedoms began to seem increasingly real, Benilde told her grandchildren stories about the past; particularly about a day in April 1939, when she was seventeen.

She was the eldest of three sisters. When they were young, their father, Waldo (short for Ubaldo) Ruíz Belmonte, had worked in the fields between Valdecaballeros and the next village, Castilblanco. They had all lived through desperate times. In 1923, soon after Benilde was born, the new military dictatorship reinforced feudalism, nowhere more strongly than in impoverished Extremadura. Foreign travellers in the region described how, if your meal included meat, you would be surrounded by sightseers while you ate it. In the winter of 1931–2, farmworkers in Castilblanco went on strike – this was when Buñuel made his Extremadura film, *Tierra sin pan* – and by the spring, they were starving. In April, during a demonstration, a member of the Guardia shot one of the strikers. Villagers turned on the police with knives and stones, killing four of them. The event caused national outrage and was a hint of what was to come.

During much of the Civil War, a portion of the front line passed between the two villages. Valdecaballeros, to the south, was taken by the nationalists and a number of families, the Ruízs among them, fled 200 kilometres eastwards to Daimiel, an important agricultural area held by the republicans. One of the main sources of food supplies for the loyalists, it was also a trade union fiefdom.

According to the stories told by Benilde, they were all too busy staying alive to take any interest in politics. When, at the end of March 1939, Franco declared victory, they assumed that the war was over and, together with their displaced neighbours, packed up such belongings as they possessed and set off for home. As the procession began to descend the mountains towards Valdecaballeros it bumped into a group of soldiers. Waldo and some of the other men were seized and taken to a prison set up in their village by the Falange, where they were kept incommunicado for three days. Whatever happened to them during that time at the hands of the celebrating victors, their ordeal ended in another journey, along the road towards Castilblanco and up a hill to what had been a republican trench, where they were shot and dumped.

For Waldo's widow, it was the end of everything. Exhausted not only by the war but, now, by obsessive speculations about why he had been killed (he had once denounced a woman in Castilblanco who had stolen two of his mules: could that have had something to do with it?), she too soon died. It was left to Benilde to look after her sisters, find a husband for herself and then bring up their own children. In the 1940s, life in Spain was not only even poorer than it had been in the 20s and 30s but, for anyone connected to someone who had fallen foul of the nationalists, it was more terrifying. Franco combined triumphalism with vindictiveness and many of those who had been killed on his own side were now exhumed and ceremonially reburied. Those associated with republicanism had to keep their heads down and their mouths shut. When Benilde finally began to tell her stories at home, though, she had a fascinated audience in Marina. At school, where the sensitive, intelligent teenager's teachers had been educated under Franco, the Civil War was hardly mentioned and this made her still more curious. She longed to do something for her grandmother; to do something about the past.

Like Marina, others in the new, European Spain were beginning to feel that history had been getting no attention, or rather, attention of the wrong kind. Monuments to the dictatorship were still to be seen everywhere: streets with the names of nationalist generals, Queipo de Llano among them; town squares dominated by equestrian statues of Franco; church porches memorializing those who had died 'for God and Spain' – as if anyone who had fought on the other side, or on none, was inevitably both an atheist and unpatriotic. This, indeed, was what Francoism had taught, especially in church. In the cathedral of Jaén, not far from where Lorca died, each of the four pillars at the transept carries a monument to clergy of the diocese killed in the Civil War: 135 are named, ranging from a bishop and other cathedral dignitaries to a monk and two men studying for ordination. Most, though, were parish priests. The murders, which were more than matched in other parts of Spain (about 6,800 clergy, monks and nuns are thought to have been killed in all, more than in the French Revolution), are an indictment of some factions of the republican movement and it's not difficult to imagine their impact in communities where priests still mattered. But the monument tells two lies. One is that the clergy died in what's described as 'the Marxist Revolution of 1936–9' – rather than as a result of a military coup supported by the Church hierarchy; the other is a lie by omission. There is no monument in the cathedral to the republican dead – to the democrats whose overthrow was called for by most of the bishops and, once accomplished, was greeted by Pope Pius XII, in a public message to Franco, 'with immense joy'.

By the 1980s and 90s, though, democracy was no longer on the losing side and there was increasing pressure for monuments to some of the more flagrant evildoers to be removed. More constructively, voluntary local associations had begun to look for ways to assist people who had suffered under the dictatorship and to make whatever public amends could be agreed. In particular, those who had been killed by the self-appointed representatives of 'God and Spain' were at last being commemorated. One of the first public signs of the change in mood came in the early 1980s, when local families supported by trade unionists put up memorials in a field close to where the Valencia –Zaragoza road passes Caudé, in the east-central province of Teruel. There was once an immense well here, eighty-four metres deep. During the Civil War, it was gradually filled with the bodies of hundreds of people executed without trial, most of them members of the Sociedad Obrera Agricola (Agricultural Workers' Union).

Partly under the influence of similar moves in areas of Latin America, families began to dig up communal graves and to give the remains a proper burial. One such exhumation was to make a far-reaching impression, including on the family of Waldo Ruíz. It took place at the beginning of the new millennium in El Bierzo, a region of León province famous for having harboured members of the post-Civil War resistance movement against Franco. The *fosa común* in question contained the remains of 'the Priaranza Thirteen', a group of militant leftists executed by members of the Falange in October 1936. The exhumation was planned by a journalist in his early thirties named Emilio Silva. At the age of ten, his father had gone from being a cheerful schoolboy to having to take responsibility for his entire family. The reason for this change of fortune was that Emilio's grandfather, an intelligent, outspoken republican who had emigrated to America but returned in 1925 to marry and start a shop in El Bierzo, was captured by the Falange and, along with the Priaranza Thirteen, shot and buried in a ditch. Like Marina and so many others born towards the end of, or soon after, Franco's lifetime, the young Emilio had grown up pondering what it must have meant for a child suddenly to become head of a Spanish family in the late 1930s.

Emilio is named after his grandfather. In *Las Fosas de Franco* – the title of the book he co-authored is difficult to translate because *fosa* means 'grave' but also 'ditch'; a proper grave is normally given a more dignified name like *tumba* or *sepultura* – he has written about his family, about his grandfather's journey in the back of a truck to the remote place where the men were to be shot, about the experience of waiting their turn and their last pleas for mercy:

> I have often thought about what must have been my grandfather's terror during those hours, about the terror of each of those men being driven to the *matadero*: fear for his own life, fear about the family he had left behind, about whether punishments would go on being inflicted on any of them. More than once I've closed my eyes and tried to put myself in my grandfather's place, to feel the same agony, the same powerlessness, the same panic.

Emilio describes his search for the grave, prompted in part by these imaginings, in part by a wish to succeed where earlier efforts by his grandmother to identify her husband's whereabouts had been officially rebuffed. The narrative is particularly vivid when he writes about what he has since learned is a common experience: that while initially survivors often seem sure where a site is, when taken there even the gravedigger may be confounded by changes in cultivation, by new buildings and roads. Trained as a sociologist, Emilio became increasingly absorbed not only in his own enquiries but in those of others with a similar emotional stake in the past. He was to be particularly influenced by the professionalism of two people who responded to an article he wrote in a local newspaper, *La Crónica de León*. They were Julio Vidal, an archaeologist whose mother came from Priaranza, and his wife, María Encina, a forensic anthropologist.

The couple had been following work in 'contemporary archaeology' which had been going on elsewhere, both in Europe, including on First World War sites in France, and in places where war crimes had been committed in more recent times, including Argentina, Rwanda and Croatia. They were familiar with the protocols that had grown up around such investigations, as well as with the use of DNA in identifying problematic remains, and had been looking for an opportunity to extend these methods to similar activities which were taking place in a more haphazard way in Spain. Both had been shocked by an exhumation in Arganza, where, a couple of years earlier, the assorted bones of half a dozen men had simply been lifted in the jaw of a mechanical digger and carted to a cemetery. Emilio was quick to enlist the couple's help and that of various other volunteers, among them a younger historian of the Civil War, Santiago Macías. All those working at Priaranza del Bierzo were passionately committed to uncovering what they saw as the truth about the Civil War. In Emilio's words, 'We were beginning to make an island of historical justice in the sea of amnesia about those who, with their ideas and with their political work, built Spain's first democracy.'

The exhumations took time. Identification of some of the remains involved lengthy archival searches as well as DNA testing. The professionalism of all this attracted attention from the media and from local politicians, and soon local authorities unanimously voted to give financial support to similar future projects in their jurisdiction. Emilio and Santiago, meanwhile, were deluged with enquiries and realized that although many regional associations were pursuing related investigations of various sorts, including in archives which are still for the most part inaccessible and poorly catalogued, there was no national forum for such work. Together, they founded what has become one of Spain's most powerful grassroots organizations: the Asociación para la Recuperación de la Memoria Histórica (ARMH).

From its reputation, you might expect the ARMH to be housed in a *palacio* somewhere near the Prado. Its activities are recorded almost every day in the Spanish media, it has an extremely efficient, informative and much-visited website – www.memoriahistorica.org – and there are more than 6,000 registered members. Emilio and Santiago have been invited to speak at international meetings of related organizations, among them the UN High Commission on Human Rights, and the association's work was to provide the Law of Historical Memory with much of its impetus. Its premises, though, consist of Emilio's small flat in a suburb of Madrid, Santiago's home in western Spain, and a van. Both men spend much of the day talking into handfuls of mobile phones. Emilio's office is a Sargasso Sea of laptops, DVDs, books, pamphlets and cuttings; Santiago is usually to be found at one site or another.

When I first met Santiago, on a bright, cold Wednesday afternoon in Valdecaballeros early in December 2008, he had come from a new project north of Cáceres, which didn't seem to be going well. He was interested in a report of a *fosa* in a small town near Guadalupe. Valdecaballeros is between the two places and Marina had recently been in touch with the association. The seventieth anniversary of Waldo's death would fall the following April. For his daughter Benilde's sake, the family hoped to mark the occasion by finding his remains and giving them a Christian burial.

We were joined by a two-man team of ground surveyors who had come from Madrid in an SUV, bringing geo-radar equipment and a metal detector. Over lunch, I asked about the expenses involved in their work. For the current set of projects there was a state subvention but the owner of the surveying business, a voluble man called Luis, said that it didn't remotely cover his costs. He grew indignant. 'If a plane crashes, there are fire engines all over the place, ambulances, Guardia. But because the Civil War dead are under the ground, *nada*. Besides, do you know what it costs to build one kilometre of *autovía*? Six million euros.' I pondered these analogies while we drove to meet a small convoy at a roundabout on the edge of the town: an elderly man in a Mercedes, Marina and her mother, Marina's sister and her boyfriend, Manuel. Benilde was staying with other relatives in Madrid.

Our route was the one along which Waldo was taken for his last ride. We parked beside the main road and, as we walked behind the surveyors' jeep up a hillside scattered with holm oaks, Waldo's great-granddaughters looked increasingly preoccupied. Here, closer to Castilblanco than Valdecaballeros, the land slopes regularly and the trees are evenly spaced. Other than a flat hilltop to the north – with its commanding views, a strategic point during the Civil War – and a Franco-era reservoir to the south, there are few distinguishing features: one patch of thistles is very like another. Halfway up, the man with the Mercedes, who turned out to be a former mayor of Valdecaballeros, said he thought the grave was on the western side of the lightly trodden path we were following. This was where the republicans had entrenched and where Waldo and the others, he believed, were buried.

Manuel, it became clear, was himself a Civil War aficionado. After some consultation, he and Santiago retraced our route and drove further along the main road, apparently to get their bearings. They returned looking decisive. On the path's eastern side, about a hundred metres from where the ex-mayor was standing, the surveyors unpacked their metal detector and a device built on what resembled a state-of-the-art baby buggy: a triangular frame on three wheels with pneumatic tyres; a plastic box slung below, containing a radar machine; on the handlebars, a monitor. Now began a slow procession over the bumpy, thorny ground, sometimes pushing the buggy, sometimes sweeping the metal detector from side to side, sometimes both. Unconvinced by this sporadic activity, the ex-mayor went home. He had told me he was doubtful about the whole procedure. Twenty years ago, there were people alive who knew everything. Now, it would be very hard to find anyone with reliable information. Besides, relatives of his had been killed on both sides. The same was true of many people around here.

Santiago spoke into his mobile. The women stood in a huddle, talking. Manuel and I took turns looking over Luis's shoulder into the monitor at oscillations which showed variations in the subsoil. He had found what he thought might be the line of the trench, which corresponded to the orientation the ex-mayor had indicated. At one point along the diagonal being surveyed, an irregular, wider, roughly triangular patch seemed to indicate a pit. Santiago marked its centre with a rock, while a few traffic cones were placed at intervals along the line.

Luis now took a turn with the metal detector and near the higher, western end of the newly marked line it began to bleep. He slid the plate above and around the spot, took out a trowel and dug. A few centimetres under the surface was a tarnished, slender bullet casing, unmistakably different from the big cartridge cases that lie everywhere in this territory of deer and wild boar hunting. He scraped off the dirt, stood the case on end, called Santiago over and carried on sweeping, while the rest of us squatted, gazing at the little exhibit. Not far off, still on the same line, Luis soon found another like it.

This was a high point of the afternoon. Another came when Santiago, confident of success now, began to ask about mechanical diggers. Catching his mood, Marina told him happily that Manuel's family had two *máquinas*. Plans for the next day were discussed – Santiago still had to go back to the dig near Cáceres – and the women left. Luis, though, was dissatisfied: 'It doesn't surprise me to find bullets where there was a military trench. I'd be happier if there were more of them.' During what remained of the sunlight, Santiago encouraged the men to work over other parts of the land, but nothing materialized. Having agreed a time to make contact later that night, we packed up, shook hands and left, Luis and his colleague going back to Madrid, Santiago to Cáceres, me to my nearby *hostal*.

In Andalucía at the beginning of the winter olive harvest, I had learned that Spanish labourers of the kind who, forty years ago, abandoned agricultural work in favour of construction are beginning to return to the land, with the result that charities are obliged to house and feed itinerant labourers from Africa who find themselves jobless. Painful cultural memories of a different kind are involved here: memories of the hungry Spain known all too well by Waldo Ruíz. I tried to imagine that time as I waited beside the Valdecaballeros–Castilblanco road, the morning after the survey, while Manuel chugged up in his yellow digger through a dense, cold mist. He was followed by Santiago in a Volkswagen people carrier and by another car also bringing volunteers – six in all, mostly in their twenties or early thirties, university-educated, some of them trained as archaeologists. In the back of the VW was a sack full of picks and trowels and also a large portable canopy, in case privacy should be needed.

At about ten-thirty, the digger made its first, cautious, half-metre-deep incision where Santiago had left his stone. Everyone stretched to stare at the pile of earth it removed, then into the hole it left. The soil was tipped gently to one side. A young woman who works full-time on ARHM digs raked through it. Nothing. Directed by an older regular member of the team, Manuel slowly repeated the process along the line marked the day before, until he had made a shallow trench about six metres long. He was then asked to go back and dig down another half-metre. This is the level at which remains are often found and, once again, the mood was expectant. Several times, one or other of the team signalled to Manuel to stop, climbed into the trench and scratched around in an area where the earth looked softer or had a different colour. When the excavation was almost two metres deep, a new one was begun, parallel to it and about a metre distant.

Any quest takes on a life of its own, becomes its own justification. Although the mood was now relaxed and jokey, everyone was bent on finding something. The team had been disappointed yesterday. Some of them had other jobs and could only join digs for a few days at a time. We were all cold and damp. Santiago was glued to his mobile when Marina and her mother and sister returned. I talked to them for some time. I wanted to hear Waldo's story from them, but realized that I was also trying to occupy them, as the digger went in and out and the volunteers raked carefully through one heap of earth, then the next.

Santiago spread some cushions on thorny ground a few metres from the excavations and produced bags of crisps and nuts. In pairs and one by one, his team broke off. A weak sun had begun to disperse the mist. Cars passing below slowed while their drivers tried to work out what was going on. Manuel filled in his two unproductive trenches and began another, then another, parallel to the first but higher up. The digger's bites were greedier now, less tentative, and were watched by fewer people.

Later that afternoon, after lunch, Santiago had time to talk to me. Born in El Bierzo in 1973, he had, as a boy, been so gripped by the stories told to him by older people that he began to record them. A particular episode, involving the lives of anti-Francoist guerrillas in a mountain hideout, was to become the subject of his prize-winning book *Los Corrales, 1942*. He had also written the accounts of almost twenty digs which make up the second part of his and Emilio Silva's *Las Fosas de Franco*. Valdecaballeros would reveal something, he said – today, tomorrow, he couldn't be sure when. The process often involved false leads, temporary disappointments. So much depended on evidence that only old people could provide. It was a pity that Benilde was still in Madrid. He had heard of a woman in the village who might know something and who would, he hoped, come to the site. The *máquina* dipped, pushed back against its haunches, scraped, pulled and reached gracefully across towards the volunteers' rakes. Everyone cursorily examined the rubber sole of a sandal *c.*1990. I followed some of the team on a walk up the hill, from the top of which you see woods, lakes, distant mountains. Scrappy modern developments surround Castilblanco and Valdecaballeros but the roads are good because they were built to serve a still-unused nuclear energy plant to the south-west. The big reservoirs are a legacy for which Franco deserves more credit than he gets. Most of the rest of what's visible must have been the same in 1939 – or 1839.

There were some movements below, around the digger. A woman had arrived – not the one Santiago was expecting but an aunt of Marina's, Benilde's only daughter. By the time I joined them, she had been arguing for some time with Marina and her mother. A hundred metres to the north-east of us, there was a low ridge. She had always heard that the grave was in the fields beyond it, closer to Castilblanco. Marina looked dejected. Manuel hunched himself over the levers in his silent cockpit. Santiago and the others wandered in different directions, some of them talking on their mobiles. Feeling like a stranger at a funeral, I moved a little way off, back up the hill. The sun had disappeared some time ago and, once again, the women set off for home. Manuel began to fill in the trenches, the volunteers folded up the unused canopy, tools were stowed back in the van. Santiago had decided to abandon Valdecaballeros until he had better information about the grave's location. They would move on to the other potential site he had mentioned, on the way to Guadalupe. Next day, after some inconclusive preliminary enquiries there, the group split up for an unexpectedly free weekend.

Marina remained in Valdecaballeros. For all the arguments I had heard and read – and in many cases sympathized with – about historical naivety and the need to focus on the future, I didn't feel like recommending her to read this or that book published twenty years ago, or to think about the economy. Anyone who met her would respect her for taking an interest, however subjective, in a cataclysm that had so much affected her family; no one could criticize her for trying to do something, however symbolic and feeble-seeming, while her grandmother was still alive. History isn't a Site of Special Scientific Interest fenced off for professional academics and intellectuals, and those who care about it, professionals as well as amateurs, are bound to bring with them the new perspectives, as well as the practical equipment, of their own generation.

Among Spain's strongest and best-known characteristics is its Moorish inheritance, visible in almost every old town, audible in the spoken language as well as in the music. Islamic Spain – Al-Andalus – has been admired, studied, romanticized, made new by people in every generation from Théophile Gautier to Lorca and since. Just as is now happening in relation to the Civil War, one 'authentic' version supersedes another and, while each myth is being picked apart and reworked, an occasional more durable element enters the cultural gene pool. I phoned Marina to check a few details: family names, numbers of siblings. Had her great-grandfather ever joined one of the farm workers' unions? She said she thought her grandmother might know, or perhaps a document could have survived. She still hoped that when Benilde was next in Valdecaballeros, she would be able to identify

Waldo's grave. I said that, if so, Santiago might try again. She replied, '*Ojalá!*'

The expression, originally Arabic, is still often heard in Spain. It used to be translated as 'God willing', but times change and today it would probably be rendered as 'If only' or 'I wish'. Etymologists point out that, strictly speaking, '*law sha'a Allah*' implies a subjunctive: 'If God were to wish it.' But what difference does it make? I said '*Ojalá!*' back. ■

POSTSCRIPT

Benilde returned to Valdecaballeros early in the new year but died unexpectedly on January 15, 2009 before any further investigation of her father's burial place could be undertaken. She was eighty-seven. In what proved to be their last conversation, Marina asked her grandmother if she had a picture of Waldo. Benilde explained that when she was a girl, people like them couldn't afford photographs.

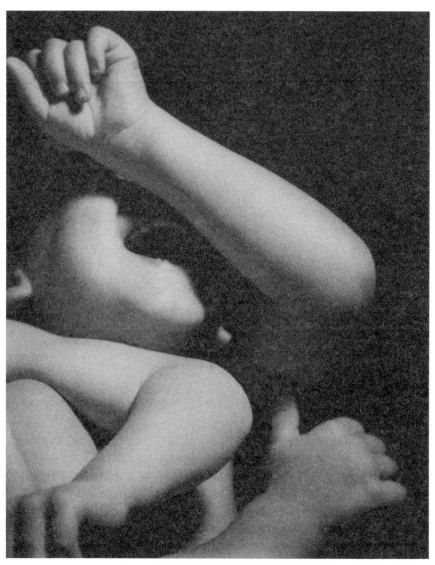

'Hals Uber Kopf' (Head over heels), 2006, by Wiebke Leister

STORY OF MY LIFE

A.L. Kennedy

I n this story, I'm like you.
Roughly and on average, I am the same: the same as you.

The same is good. The same is that for which we're meant. It's comforting and gently ties us, makes us unified and neat and it tells us the most pleasant kinds of story, the ones that say how beautifully we fit, the ones that summon up their own attention, make us look.

I understand this.

I understand a lot – very often – almost all the time – most especially the stories. They are an exercise of will: within them whatever I think, I can wish it to be. They are the worlds that obey me, kinder and finer worlds: in many of them, for example, I'd have no teeth.

Because I believe I'd do better with a beak. So why not have one? That shouldn't be impossible. I feel a beak could make me happy, quite extraordinarily content: sporting something dapper and useful in that line – handy for cracking walnuts, nipping fingers, tweezing seeds. Not that I've ever fancied eating seeds, but one can't predict the path of appetite.

And beaks come in different sizes: that's a plus, along with the range of designs. The toucan would be good for parties, shouting, grievous bodily harm. Ibis: mainly funerals and plumbing. Sparrow: best for online dating and eating crisps. The options, while not infinite, are extensive. In a reasonable world my personality would give rise to my true beak, would nurture it, my proper fit – parrot, hummingbird, bullfinch, albatross – and through it I'd express myself, be jauntily apparent, fulfilled, really start going somewhere with my whole appearance – somewhere free from teeth – somewhere other than the dentist.

Story of my life – maybe – going to the dentist.

Because my teeth, they've always been ambitious, problematic, expansive. I never have had enough room for all of them and so out they've come: milk teeth, adult teeth, wisdom teeth. Handfuls of them over the years, practically a whole piano's worth. Of course, when I was a kid they still gave you gas for extractions – general, potentially fatal, anaesthetic gas administered, in my case, by an elderly man with unhygienically hairy ears who would bend in at me, eerily grinning, and exclaim – every single time – 'Good Lord, dearie, they're some size, those teeth,' while he flourished that black rubber mask and then cupped me under it, trapped my mouth in one hard, chilly pounce: 'Breathe deeply, dearie. Count backwards from ten.'

I'd shut my eyes and picture his tufted, werewolf earlobes and count until I'd reached as far as seven or so before I'd see these angles of tilting grey that folded in towards a centre point, bolted and sleeked at the backs of my eyes and then rolled me down and away to the dark.

Now, as it happens, I'm not good with chemicals. No choice here – I am made the way I'm made. Sensitive.

In the chair they'd give me nitrous oxide and it put me out nicely enough. I'd swim deep through a cartoony, bendy blank while the dentist did his work – the tugging, the twists – then I'd float straight back up and just bob at the surface like a tiny shore-leave sailor: changeable and land sick and absolutely smashed.

My first experience of the freedom within incapacity. That swoop and rock and thunder of delight. It's always best to meet your pleasures before you can tell what they mean.

As I came round some nurse would be attending with her kidney dish and towels: a bit broody perhaps, protective – the motherly type but not a mother and therefore idealistic, if not ridiculous, about kids. She would, shall we say, not entirely expect the violence of my post-operative dismay: my tiny swinging fists and my confusion, my not unjustifiable sense of loss.

I have no idea what I shouted on these occasions – a small person turning expansive, losing it, throwing it, swarming clear out into beautiful rage. I'll pretend, while I tell you the story, that I know.

I'll say I produced – at great speed and with feeling – 'You get away from me! I'll have you! I'll set the Clangers on you. And Bagpuss! Taking my teeth out...no one ever takes *me* out – except to the dentist – to take out more teeth. I need my teeth for the tooth fairy – I'm only five, for Chrissake – that's my one source of income, right there. How else can I save up to run away from here? I could go on the stage – be a sideshow – my manager would want me absolutely as I am – *The Shark Tooth Girl: the more you pull, the more she grows: ivory from head to toes.* I'd be laughing. With all of my teeth, I'd be laughing.'

This is untrue, but diagnostic – it helps to make me plain.

Because I wouldn't ever want to hide from you.

The surprise of my own blood, that's true – thick and live and oddly tasty – I never did get used to that, my inside being outside – on my face, my hands. Even today, if I take a tumble, suffer a lapse, my blood can halt and then amaze me. It's almost hypnotic – seeing myself run. And persons of my type, we run so easily: bird's hearts thumping in us and broad veins full of shocks.

Back from the surgery, next came the hangover – naturally, naturally, naturally – but as I was a child it would be kind, more a mild type of fog than a headache. Beyond it I'd be given soldiers with soft-boiled eggs, gentle food for an affronted mouth and a sudden hunger – oh, such a lively hunger – and a quiet mother comfort to meet it with a little spoon. Then a bath and an early night pelting with lurid dreams of thieves and tunnels and running for my life, right through my life and out the other side and into nowhere: the coppery taste of absence, liquid heat.

Once I was older, I decided I had no more time to waste – people to do and things to be – and avoiding the dental issue became attractive. I brushed regularly, kept my head down, ate everything wholemeal for added wear, but it did no good: my teeth are forceful. They insist.

So when I'm twenty-four, twenty-five, I'm back in the surgery – new dentist – and the first of my wisdom teeth is leaving. Local anaesthetic this time, much more practical and safe, and I haven't enjoyed the injections, but I'm hoping they'll do the trick – mostly my eye's gone a little blurry, but that's nothing to fret about – and here comes the dentist – big man, meaty forearms, substantial grip – and it's plain that he'll check now, tap about to see if I'm numb and therefore happy – except he doesn't. He does not.

And I should pause here briefly, because it lets the story breathe and even possibly give a wink. I step back to let you step forward and see what's next. This way you'll stay with us. With me.

Which is the point.

You staying with me is the point.

And, no, the dentist doesn't check, he is incurious and generally impatient, goes at it fiercely with the pliers and no preamble and here comes a clatter, a turning yank, and then tooth – I am looking at my tooth without me, grinning redly in the light – and I am puzzled because of this feeling, this building feeling which I cannot quite identify – it is large, huge, and therefore moving rather slowly, takes a full *count backwards from tennineeight* to arrive and then I know, then I am wholly, supernaturally aware, I am certain in my soul that I'm in pain. This is hitherto unguessed-at pain – pain of the sort I have tried to anticipate and forestall with insulating activities and assistance. Numb is best – I always aim for numb, for numb of any type – but pain has found me anyway. Worse than imagination, here it is.

To be fair, the dentist was upset – looking down at me and saying, 'Oh dear' a number of times before offering a seat in his office and an explanation involving wrongly positioned nerves – it was technically my fault for having provided them. His secretary gave me a comforting and yet excruciating cup of tea.

I walked home – it wasn't far – dizzy and racing with adrenalin. They put it in the anaesthetic, presumably to give it extra zip. Which is to say that you go to the dentist – somebody worrying – and he then injects you with terror – pure fear – you feel it rush your arms, cup its lips hard over that bird inside your chest.

And it is possibly, conceivably, odd that this is so familiar, so really exactly the simple jolt of many mornings, and you draw near to your house and wonder, as usual, if so much anxiety should not have a basis in fact. Perhaps a leak under your floorboards has caused rot, perhaps you're ill – genuinely threatened by what, as soon as they knew you weren't suing, your dentist and his secretary called *a head injury* – this making you feel very noble for not complaining, but nevertheless in many ways it sounds dire. And if you really want to fret, then perhaps you shouldn't lend that guy your money – your guy, your money, but shouldn't they still be apart? You like them both but they should surely be apart? And what if he isn't exclusively your guy; you've had that unease, felt that whisper, about him before – and it's screaming today. And what if your life is, in some degree, wrong or maladjusted when hauling a live tooth raw from the bone leaves you and your state no worse than an average night, a convivial night, a pace or two along your path of joy.

Sensitivity, you see? It causes thoughts.

When I reached the flat, I let myself in and sat on the sofa, hands holding each other to dampen their shake and keep out the sense of having gone astray: twenty-five and no real profession, no prudent strategy, not much of a relationship.

And too many teeth.

But you try to keep cheery, don't you? And you have time. At twenty-five you've bags of it.

Thirty-five, that's a touch more unnerving – wake up with thirty-five and you'll find that it nags, expects things you don't have: kitchen extensions and dinner parties, DIY, the ability to send out Christmas cards signed *With love from both of us. With love from all of us.*

Instead I'm house-sitting for friends.

And this section of the story is here for you to like and to let your liking spread to me. Frailty and failure, they're charismatic, they have a kind of nakedness that charms.

So.

Minding the house is company for me.

Well, it *isn't* company – the owners are obviously away, hence my minding – and they've left their cats. And this is domesticity without effort: Brazilian cleaning lady, leather cushions, large numbers of superfluous and troubling ornaments.

This isn't like me owning cats, me living alone with cats, me growing six-inch fingernails and giggling through the letter box when the pizza delivery man comes, peering out at him and smelling of cats – that's not how it is.

There are these other people who are not me and they are the ones who have the cats and I am treating their animals politely but with an emotional distance, no dependency and no indications of despair. There should be no suggestion that these friends are sorry for me, that the husband is more sorry than the wife and that they have argued about my trustworthiness in their absence and their possessions and have doubted the supervisory skills of a Portuguese-speaking obsessive-compulsive who polishes their every surface twice a week: tables, glasses, apples, door knobs, the skin between the end of the air and the beginning of my wine. I will not tell you that they left behind them a plethora of mildly hysterical notes, or that their act of charity has been overshadowed by a sense of filth, oncoming sadness.

It is only important to mention that I was, on this particular house-sitting evening, chipper and at ease. I had fed both of the creatures and I was going out – out on a date – a variation on a theme of what could be a date. We had reached a transitional stage, the gentleman and I – which is to say, I had reached it and wondered if he had too – and I have to make the best of what I may get, so I was dressed presentably and poised to be charming and, had it not been for the stitches in my mouth, I would have been perfectly on form.

More dentistry – surgical dentistry, but with mouthwash and antibiotics and painkillers – big ones.

I like them big.

So I'm all right.

I'm stylish.

And I slip into the restaurant – once I've found it – with what I consider to be grace and it's an agreeable establishment. Italian. So I can have pasta – which is soft.

And here's my date – my approaching-a-date – and he's looking terrific.

He's looking great. Like a new man.

Truly amazing.

He's looking practically as if he's someone else.

Yes.

Yes, he is.

He is someone else.

I am waving at someone else. The man I am meeting is sitting behind him and to the left and not waving. No one, to be accurate, *is* waving apart from me and I would love to stop waving, but have been distracted by the expression on my almost-date's face.

He is experiencing emotions which will not help me.

But I can still save the evening. I'm a fighter. I calmly and quietly explain the particular story which is presently myself: the drugs I am currently taking – prescribed drugs – the residual levels of discomfort, the trouble I have enunciating – and perhaps he might like to tell me about *his* week and I can listen.

People like it when you listen.

They have stories, too.

But he doesn't give me anything to hear.

And so I talk about my roots – *that* story – a little bit angry, because he should have been better than he is, should have been a comfort. My roots are twenty-three millimetres long, which is not unimpressive, is almost an inch. I tell him about my root canals. I summarize the activities involved in an apesectomy – the gum slicing, the tissue peeling, the jaw drilling, the noise.

This is not romantic, because I no longer wish to be, not any more. I am watching a space just above his head and to the right where another part of my future is closing, folding into nowhere, tasting coppery and hot.

Could be worse, though: could be forty-five, when everything tilts and greys and comes to point behind your eyes and you have not run away, you have waited for the world to come towards you, given it chance after chance. And, besides this, you find it difficult to name what else you have done, or who is yours. After so many years you are aware of certain alterations, additions, the ones that would make you like everyone else, that would join you, tie you gently, allow you to fit.

But they don't make a story – they're only a list.

More dental adventure, that'll keep us right – another practice, another extraction, another tale to tell and that remaining wisdom tooth: it's shy, it lacks direction, the time has come to cut it out.

Cheery dentist, in this instance, talkative. 'This is an extremely straightforward operation. It is, of course, *oral surgery*, but you'll be fully anaesthetized.' Which is frankly the least I would hope and dialogue, that's always a boon – a voice beyond my own, someone in whom I can believe.

He puts his needle in. 'There we are...' and the numbness goes up to my eye. Again. Faulty wiring. So my mouth is now more painful than it was and I'm also half blind. 'Well, I'll just deal with that, then – there you go.'

Oh, that's better, that is good. Thass gread.

And this is my speaking voice, my out-loud voice, the one for everyone but you. *So it's in italics* – that way you'll know.

Thass bedder. Thass suffithiently aneasssetithed. You may protheed.

When we're in private – like now – and I say this to no one but you, then italics are unnecessary.

We can be normal and alone.

'No, I think you need more than that.'

And this is where the dentist gives me more anaesthetic and I notice his hands smell a little like cornflakes – his gloves, they have this cornflaky scent – which is a detail that makes him seem credible and not simply a nightmare.

'Perhaps a touch more there.'

Whad? No, no, thass a bid mush.

'And some more.'

Shurly nod?

'And more than that. Splendid.'

I can'd feed by arms.

'Of course, the effects of the anaesthetic will usually pass after three or four hours. But working so close to a nerve as well, in very unusual patients the numbness will pass in three or four...'

It would be tiresome to pause here.

So we won't.

'...months and in some extraordinary cases, you will be like that... for the rest of your life.'

Ffnd?

'Here we go then.'

It's not that I don't appreciate the chance to feel nothing at all – but this isn't that – this is horror combined with paralysis – only very minutely exaggerated paralysis. I can't see to hit him, I can't fight him off and he's digging and drilling, drilling and digging, and the extraction takes forty-five minutes.

Honestly.

That's how long it takes – no exaggeration.

There's blood in his hair.

It's mine.

Finally, I'm released, it's over, the stitches have been stitched, and I run out of the surgery.

Well, I pay the bill and I run out of the surgery.

Well, I pay the bill and ask them to call me a cab and I run out of the surgery.

Well, I can't really run, but I leave the surgery as best I can and I wait for the cab in what happens to be a colourful urban area, one where relaxed gentlemen stroll the boulevards of an afternoon and possibly sing. Perhaps there may be vomit on a lapel here and there. Perhaps there may be vomit and no lapel. And I'm standing – just about – and I can hear a relaxed gentleman coming along behind me.

He says something approaching, 'Hhaaaaa.' Which is not much of a story, but is true and I know what he means because I can speak alcoholic. I have learned.

He reaches me and he says what might be expected – ''Scuse me cunyou spare twenny pence furra cuppa tea.' And I turn to him with my bleeding mouth and my lazy eye and my dodgy arm and my swollen tongue and I say, 'I don no. Havin a biddofa bad day mysel.'

So he gave me twenty pence.

And a slightly used sweet.

And a kiss.

It's best, if you can, to close up every story with a kiss.

If you can.

Story of my life – maybe – going to the dentist.

The story that kept you here with me and that was true. In its essentials it was never anything other than true.

True as going to sleep tonight with the idea of blood beneath my tongue and meeting the old dreams of robbery and tunnels, the ones where I run straight through and beyond myself and on. And sometimes I wake up sore and wanting to set out nice fingers of bread and runny egg and avoiding the issue is always attractive, but I am tired of speaking languages that no one understands and I have only these words and no others and this makes my stories weak, impossible – impossible as the Christmas cards – *with love from all of us* – the night hugs and pyjamas, the tantrums and the lost shoes and the hoarding of eccentric objects – figurines, sea glass, washers – which are the kinds of details that should not be discussed. They are impossible as hiding the so many ways that my insides leak out, show in my hands, my face.

Impossible as telling you a story of a new arrival – a small person, turning expansive – someone growing and beautiful, but not perfect, the story of their first trip to the dentist, their first real fear I'd want to drive away. My duty would be to ensure that we would conquer, because every pain is survivable, although it may leave us different, more densely ourselves. The child and I, we would be unafraid and we'd have stories and every one of them would start with:

In this story, you are not like me.

All of my life I'll take care we are never the same. ∎

AMONG THE PIPEMEN

In spite of fashion and a smoking ban,
the 'brotherhood of the briar' proves
largely unflappable

Andrew Martin

A s a boy I owned, and kept in a drawer containing my personal
treasures, a pamphlet entitled *Pipes and Pipemen*. On the cover was
a drawing of a bouffant-haired man (this was the mid-Seventies) puffing
on a pipe with eyes half-closed in rapture. Inside was some purple stuff
about 'the pleasures of the briar', followed by a list of all the men who'd
won the Pipe Smoker of the Year award. I knew some of these men, and
their pipes, from watching children's television. There was the bucolic
broadcaster Jack Hargreaves (Pipe Smoker of the Year 1969), who was
apparently a very important player at Southern Television, but who was
always dressed as though about to go fly-fishing. When, as a panellist on
the programme *How!*, it was his turn to explain some scientific curiosity
to his audience of eight- to fourteen-year-olds, there would be a good
few seconds of preliminary pipe-puffing – very relaxing for Jack, but
very tense-making for us children as we fretted: 'Is he ever going to take
that thing out of his mouth and begin?'

Then there was the cricketer and professional Yorkshireman Fred
Trueman (Pipe Smoker of the Year 1974), who fronted a teatime

programme called Indoor League. Trueman presented this show – a children's programme, I repeat – from a pub, while drinking a pint of beer and smoking a pipe, and the opening shot showed him doing these things in profile, apparently perfectly content, so that when he turned and faced the camera (in order to introduce games of darts, shove ha'penny and pub skittles), he did so with an air of great magnanimity or, indeed, martyrdom.

My Uncle Sid smoked a pipe. He maximized the soothing, ritualistic aspects of the process in that he not only wielded the pipe cleaners, the various prodding instruments of a pipe tool and the weathered, old-faithful tobacco pouch, but he also rubbed his own tobacco, which came out of the tin solid, like a little piece of card. When these preliminaries were complete, and the flame was lowered on to the tobacco, there was what seemed like a crisis (not that Uncle Sid was remotely unsettled) as he discharged great clouds of smoke in the opening moments of combustion. This, to me, was as time-hallowed, as wholly masculine and right, as seeing a steam locomotive getting going. And in fact Uncle Sid *was* a train driver, and it was the contrast between his man of action persona – he was also a keen gardener – and the state he fell into with the pipe properly lit that I found particularly attractive. When Uncle Sid's pipe was up and running, so to speak, then the smoke streams issuing from him were almost invisible, and he seemed to exist in a different dimension. He might be *referred to* by those present (especially, and in rather aggrieved tones, by his own wife), but he hardly ever participated in the conversation himself. Well, he didn't need to: he had his pipe.

On those occasions when my father took me into pubs, I would focus on the Uncle Sid types, with their pipes in their mouths and their pipe paraphernalia on the table before them, forming a barricade between them and the outside world. The pipe was so obviously the priority with these men that I would wonder how those in their company could put up with being marginalized in that way. But I was on the side of the pipemen. Objectively, you might say they were under-weaned, but to me their pipes symbolized maturity and achievement. Pipes were not dashing or rakish, as cigars were in the nineteenth century and cigarettes in the twentieth; they were for men who'd graduated beyond trying to be 'cool', and I admired that, perhaps because I stood on the foothills of trying to be cool myself, and I knew it was going to be a hard slog.

I wanted, some day, to escape into the dreamworld the pipe smokers inhabited. I wanted the sure, steadfast companionship of a pipe (as I believe my pamphlet had it). That would solve the problem of what luxury I would select when invited on to the radio programme *Desert Island Discs*. 'I would like my pipe, if I may, Roy... [the presenter was Roy Plomley in those days]. Or might I be cheeky and ask for my whole collection of pipes?' I would one day feature on the programme, perhaps for my achievements in farming, since I wanted to be a farmer. I also aspired to be a Pipe Smoker of the Year. My only reservation about pipe smoking was that, since you didn't inhale, it carried a taint of cowardice compared with cigarette smoking. But I felt that, having paid my dues with a couple of decades of cigarette smoking, I would be entitled (if still alive) to graduate to the more tranquil realm of the pipe.

I am forty-six now, and it would be age-appropriate for me to start smoking a pipe, especially since I've been limbering up with cigarettes and cigars for years. But I can't be Pipe Smoker of the Year, since the award has fallen foul of the ban on promoting smoking. It was given for the last time in 2004, when it was won by somebody from the tobacco industry that no layman has heard of. The last celebrity winner was Stephen Fry, in 2003. Fry is a genuine pipe smoker all right, and he sometimes goes so far as to appear on television with a pipe in his mouth, although of course it remains unlit.

Since the ban on smoking in public places, the pipe smokers that I used to see inside pubs are now outside pubs, often standing in the rain. But such is the sanguine nature of the pipe smoker that their feathers seem to have been only slightly ruffled and they appear to be keeping up with the times. I saw one dandyish figure outside the Swan hotel in Southwold, Suffolk, who was puffing on a great saxophone of a pipe (a Sherlock Holmes) while frowning over his BlackBerry. He was only in his thirties, too, so new blood is apparently coming through. I approached another man, of similar age, who was smoking a pipe outside the Gatehouse pub in Highgate in London. Why a pipe? I asked him. 'Well,' he eventually drawled, because he had the fascinating latency of all pipemen, even at ten o'clock on a freezing night, 'I saw some good-quality ones for sale on eBay, and I think it's more interesting than a cigarette... Safer, too.'

'With cigarettes,' an assistant at the tobacconists J.J. Fox of St James's Street airily pronounced when I visited the shop, 'I suppose it's the lungs.' (Yes, I thought, that would be the problem, along with numerous other organs.) 'Whereas with a pipe,' he continued, 'you don't inhale.' He said that because the smoking of cigarettes had been so demonized, a steady trickle of smokers were taking to pipes as a more civilized and safer alternative. But this trickle of aspirational cigarette smokers has always existed and, from pipe tobacco duty figures he'd seen, he reckoned that the number of pipe smokers in Britain was down to 'just over two hundred thousand'.

I told him that I was proposing to join their number, but he didn't exactly clasp my hand in enthusiastic welcome. Instead, he gestured to one side of the plush, library-like premises, towards a display of pipes covering an entire wall. Intimidated, I asked him to pick one for me – a cheap one, since some cost hundreds of pounds. The one he chose was basically straight-stemmed but with a slight curvature 'to break the tension', or to take the weight off the teeth. It cost thirty pounds and was called a Billiard. This struck me as a beautiful name, but then the names of all types of pipe are redolent of seasoned soundness: Apple, Saddle Horn, Bulldog, Liverpool, Dublin, Prince. I asked the assistant to recommend a tobacco and he picked out Kentucky Nougat: 'It's light, won't burn your tongue, and it's got a Madagascan vanilla running through it.' Overwhelmed by the exoticism, I agreed. I was thinking of going for the full 'Uncle Sid', namely: tobacco pouch, pipe tool and lighter, but the assistant advised, 'Wait and see if you like it first.' This man, although polite, could certainly not be accused of promoting smoking. When I asked for some tips on pipe-smoking technique, he referred me to the Internet. He did, however, offer me the address of the Pipe Club of London which, he said, had formerly been one of dozens of pipe-smoking clubs operating under the auspices of a parent body, the Pipe Club of Great Britain. But the parent is now dead and only about half a dozen of its offspring remain.

Any account of contemporary pipe smoking must be replete with such diminuendos. J. J. Fox, for instance, is one of only a handful of tobacconists left in central London, where before there'd been about forty. Holding open the door of Fox's for me, the assistant said, 'I used to service J. B. Priestley at Wix's on Piccadilly – next to the naughty cinema. It's a tourist shop now. He was a grumpy old bastard.' Priestley (Pipe Smoker of the Year 1979) smoked several pipes while lying in a hot bath every morning. 'Like many of my idle, daydreaming, egotistical tribe,' he wrote, 'I am a heavy pipe smoker.' (He was speaking of writers, at a time when a pipe was a literary prop second only to the pen.)

The Pipe Club of Great Britain was founded in 1969, the Pipe Club of London in 1970. Back then, one man in seven smoked a pipe. Actually, this is another diminuendo since, at the beginning of the twentieth century, *four-fifths* of the tobacco smoked in Britain had been smoked in a pipe, but one in seven was a healthy enough figure, if healthy is quite the right word.

In 1970 the government was still a year away from discreetly printing on tobacco products: WARNING BY HM GOVERNMENT, SMOKING CAN DAMAGE YOUR HEALTH, though the link between smoking and lung cancer had been officially accepted as far back as 1955. Then again, the prime minister during the first half of 1970 was Harold Wilson (Pipe Smoker of the Year 1976), who paraded his pipe smoking, knowing that it indicated reliability and industriousness. In his excellent *Faber Book of Smoking*, James Walton quotes George Gissing: 'A pipe for the hour of work; a cigarette for the hour of conception; a cigar for the hour of vacuity.' (The contrast with Priestley's remarks above is instructive. Pipe smokers see themselves as both practically competent and philosophical. They keep their heads when all about them are losing theirs. Two pipe smokers, quite independently, offered me the following homily: 'If you go into an office and you want something done, look for the chap smoking a pipe' – an option that is unfortunately no longer available.)

In private, Wilson smoked a more plutocratic cigar. But he scored a smoking 'full house' in that he recommended the bookending of a pipe-smoking session by the smoking of two cigarettes. These would point up the superior flavour of the pipe. He can be seen advocating this in footage on YouTube which is entitled *Harold Wilson, Pipesmoker Extraordinaire*, even though his pipe appears to go out about half a dozen times during the five-minute clip. Evidently, the mere fact of a man smoking a pipe is now a spectacle in itself.

The history of the Pipe Club of London is documented in the back numbers of the journal *Pipe Line* (RIP: 1990). In 1970, a pipe-smoking competition was held between the club and Cambridge University Smoking Society. Among the contestants was the BBC Radio 1 DJ Ed 'Stewpot' Stewart (oddly he was never Pipe Smoker of the Year), who 'achieved the best time of fifty-seven minutes'. A word of explanation here. There's lately been much righteous anger about tobacco sponsorship of sports events, sport being deemed incompatible with smoking, but for a long time pipe smoking *was* a sport, of sorts. A skilled pipe smoker can keep a full pipe of tobacco burning for about an hour, although the world record is more like three hours.

On November 10, 1973 – according to *Pipe Line* – the first, and last, pipe-smoking stand-off between the Pipe Club of London and the Pipe Club of Australia was held. Qantas Airways supplied a radio link, and the London men smoked in the boardroom of Alfred Dunhill, tobacconists, in Jermyn Street, while the Australians smoked in a pub somewhere in Australia (the exact location is not recorded). It was felt at the time that the Australians had the benefit of a more relaxed environment; including the availability of beer and the fact that it was Friday evening their time, as opposed to nine-thirty on Saturday morning in London. Many pipe-smoking competitions have been discontinued owing to the difficulty of finding a venue. And the smoking ban caused membership of the Pipe Club of London to drop from about 600 to about 300, although the figures are rising slowly again.

My first contact with the club was via a long-standing, indeed honorary, member, Mr William Ashton-Taylor, who runs one of the last half-dozen pipe-manufacturing firms in Britain. At one point, Mr Ashton-Taylor, who is in his sixties and somehow has the perfect name for a pipe manufacturer, employed twelve people. But he is now a 'one-man band' and makes his pipes in a workshop at the bottom of his garden.

He inhabits a large villa in Essex and, as he served me a mug of tea, I decided he had all the characteristics of a pipe smoker. The plush, silent Jaguar in which he'd collected me from the railway station seemed a pipe smoker's car par excellence, and Mr Ashton-Taylor was dapper, calm and personable, all of which seemed quite appropriate for a pipeman. He had the hypnotic latency too, as I discovered when he asked to see the pipe I'd bought. He picked it up and took it over to a sidelight in his kitchen, the better to examine it. He turned it over and over, sighing slightly. When he returned it to me, he said, 'Well, I'd say the person who sold you that did so in good faith. It's not a bad pipe.' But the grain of the briar as seen on the bowl did not swirl as densely as he would have liked. 'They've used a filler, you see, so it doesn't look so good, and there'll be some loss of heat.' This was a question of money. The more you spend, the more grain you get.

Mr Ashton-Taylor proposed walking the length of his garden to the workshop but was very concerned that my suede shoes would get wet, which I thought a very pipe-smokerly thing to be concerned *about*.

In his workshop, I was confronted with the evolution of the briar pipe in all its various stages, ranging from pipes still looking rather tree branch-like, to those half-carved and crudely approximating to the finished article, to the finished articles themselves, in different states of smoothness and refinement. I asked Mr Ashton-Taylor how many pipefuls of tobacco he smoked a day and he replied, 'Oh, I don't

smoke. Well, maybe a cigar at Christmas.' A *cigar*? At *Christmas*? 'I just
never got the habit,' he said. So I had to conclude that Mr Ashton-
Taylor had all the characteristics of a pipe smoker except that of
actually smoking a pipe.

He has made pipes smoked by the above-mentioned Harold
Wilson and Stephen Fry, as well as the flautist James Galway and the
boxer Henry Cooper (Pipe Smoker of the Year in 1981 and 1984
respectively). His pipes are all handmade from the finest briar, which
is not, incidentally, the prickly bush of the wild rose, as found in
England, but the *Erica arborea*, an evergreen shrub of southern Europe
– and pipes are carved not from its branches but its roots.

Mr Ashton-Taylor began his working life as a lathe turner at
Dunhill. The company taught him 'how to make pipes from start to
finish by hand', and he suggested that he might display the art by
working in the shop windows of various branches of Dunhill. He then
struck out on his own. His pipes are now sold to connoisseurs rather
than to the casual pipeman – a category that hardly exists, now that the
brotherhood of the briar is so small and beleaguered. Most of his
customers have many pipes. 'They'll come up to one of my stands at
a smokers' event and their wives will be saying to me, "But he's already
got a pipe." "Yes," I'll say, "and he wants *another*." ' His tone had gone
rather steely as he recounted that dialogue, but Mr Ashton-Taylor
believes he has 'saved many marriages' by recommending that the man
smoke aromatic tobacco.

After the tour of his workshop, Mr Ashton-Taylor drove me
a couple of miles in the Jag to the Thatcher's Arms in Great Warley, a
dark, oak-beamed pub where the Pipe Club of London has found
a refuge and a venue for its monthly meetings, having been exiled from
a pub in Holborn that 'didn't want smokers anywhere near it' after the
ban came in. Were it not for the sight of a chap using a mobile phone
in the inglenook, one might almost have thought that clay pipes would
be for hire behind the bar, as they would have been in any eighteenth-
century coaching inn, the end of the stem being snapped off – in the
interests of hygiene – for each successive user. Of course, the pub does

not permit smoking inside, and Mr Ashton-Taylor showed me the open-sided wooden smoking booth the landlord had created in the backyard. It bore the insignia of both Ashton-Taylor Pipes and the Pipe Club of London. 'Not bad, is it?' said Mr Ashton-Taylor. 'Thirteen grand the landlord spent on that.'

The club would be convening within it in ten days' time. Mr Ashton-Taylor urged me attend – 'This is where all the action happens' – and I undertook to do so.

I realized that, in order to hold my own in that booth, the epicentre of British pipe smokership, I had better work on my smoking technique. But where to light up? Certainly, I was banned from smoking in my own home. So I found myself, pipe in hand, in a wooden shelter overlooking the sea at Southwold, where we have a weekend bolt-hole. The shelter was open at the front and the sides, and so was more outdoors than indoors, and there was a nasty crosswind that threatened to affect my loading of the pipe with tobacco, let alone the lighting of it.

I took the tobacco and put it, half gently, half firmly, into the bowl. I was trying to follow the maxim quoted by Georges Herment, hero of the French Resistance, jazz enthusiast and author of the classic pipe smoker's apologia, *The Pipe* (1954): 'Fill your pipe firstly with a child's hand, then a woman's, then a man's.' Easier said than done of course, but the aim is to have the tobacco loose at the bottom of the bowl, to facilitate an easy draw, then more tightly packed above, so as to prevent the overheating that results from *too* easy a draw.

The loading completed, I reached self-consciously for my matches. Two birdwatchers sat ten feet along from me in the shelter. Muffled in thick coats, they looked out to sea through binoculars. The first of the pair was more upbeat, or possibly naive, than the other. 'Wader at twelve o'clock,' he said, as I lowered my match into the tobacco. 'Right,' the second man unenthusiastically replied, as the tobacco failed to take. (Not to worry. I had read that the first match seldom does the job.) I introduced a second match as the first birdwatcher suggested, 'Might

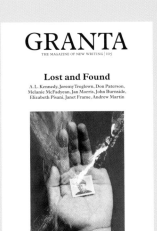

Gift subscription offer: take out an annual subscription as a gift and you will also receive a complimentary *Granta* special-edition MOLESKINE® notebook

GIFT SUBSCRIPTION 1

Address:

TITLE: INITIAL: SURNAME:

ADDRESS:

POSTCODE:

TELEPHONE:

EMAIL:

GIFT SUBSCRIPTION 2

Address:

TITLE: INITIAL: SURNAME:

ADDRESS:

POSTCODE:

TELEPHONE:

EMAIL:

YOUR ADDRESS FOR BILLING

TITLE: INITIAL: SURNAME:

ADDRESS:

POSTCODE:

TELEPHONE: EMAIL:

NUMBER OF SUBSCRIPTIONS	DELIVERY REGION	PRICE	
☐	UK	£34.95	All prices include delivery
☐	Europe	£39.95	YOUR TWELVE-MONTH SUBSCRIPTION
☐	Rest of World	£45.95	WILL INCLUDE FIVE ISSUES

I would like my subscription to start from:

☐ the current issue   ☐ the next issue

PAYMENT DETAILS

☐ I enclose a cheque payable to '*Granta*' for £ _____ for _____ subscriptions to *Granta*

☐ Please debit my ☐ MASTERCARD ☐ VISA ☐ AMEX for £ _____ for _____ subscriptions

NUMBER ☐☐☐☐ ☐☐☐☐ ☐☐☐☐ ☐☐☐☐   SECURITY CODE ☐☐☐

EXPIRY DATE ☐☐ / ☐☐   SIGNED _____   DATE _____

☐ Please tick this box if you would like to receive special offers from *Granta*
☐ Please tick this box if you would like to receive offers from organizations selected by *Granta*

Please return this form to: **Granta Subscriptions, PO Box 2068, Bushey, Herts, WD23 3ZF, UK, call Freephone 0500 004 033** or go to **www.granta.com**

Please quote the following promotion code when ordering online: **GBIUK105**

be a bit...long-necked?' 'Nah,' the second man was saying as I puffed
at my pipe, alarmed at the great gouts of blue smoke streaming from
it and me. 'Bog standard, that is.'

The pair must often have shared the shelter with pipe smokers, I
decided, as I began blowing thinner streams of smoke in a more
urbane manner. Southwold is that sort of place. At any rate, they had
not so far paid me any attention. My pipe went out again as the second
man gloomily enquired, 'Nothing doing yesterday, I suppose?' 'There
was a chiffchaff calling all the time,' the first man brightly offered, as I
puffed the thing into life again. I was then vouchsafed a further five
minutes of mellow pipe smoking, in which the second man tried to
make out that the chiffchaff had in fact been a bullfinch, and as such
nothing to write home about. The tobacco had a creamy, moreish
savour, wholly superior to any cigarette I had ever tasted. I began to
relax. I left the pipe out of my mouth for five seconds...ten... I realized
that I did not have to concentrate absolutely on it, but could take it for
granted and look out to sea, towards where the optimistic birdwatcher
was pointing and saying, 'Just there, about two o'clock...'

And then my pipe went out. I tried to light it again; it went out
again. I tried three more times without success. In annoyance, I bashed
it against the bench and the contents of the bowl spilled out. It is
permissible to leave a bit of unsmoked tobacco – the dottle – but about
half of mine was unsmoked. I kicked in frustration at the mound of
baccy and walked out of the shelter. If the two birdwatchers had
noticed that today's pipe smoker was a little less well balanced than the
usual sort, they gave no sign of the fact, the first one merely trying to
interest the second one in a sighting of 'about a hundred and fifty
starlings and a few skylarks'.

The Thatcher's Arms, a week later, was a vision of a country pub
in the Fifties, only more so. The place was full of men walking
about with pipes between their teeth. Except that it was like one of
those puzzles: 'What is missing from this picture?' The answer: smoke.
William Ashton-Taylor was present, at a table of his pipes for sale in

velvet-lined cases. He had put on a pinstriped double-breasted suit to be commensurately smart.

I walked into the backyard of the pub to the smoking shelter, which was occupied by eight or nine men. There was perhaps an above-average incidence of facial hair, and of waistcoats. A distinguished-looking, grey-bearded man was puffing on a pipe (well, they were *all* doing that) and saying, in patrician tones, 'This is Aylesbury Latikia blend. John's given me a taste of it and it's really rather good.'

The speaker was Patrick Brain, a Methodist minister from Walthamstow, known to his flock as 'the smoking vicar'. As I set about filling my own pipe, the assembly had moved on to the question of throwing old pipes away, which hardly any of them ever did. 'The only pipe I've thrown away,' said Patrick Brain, gently puffing, 'was the one I was smoking when my wife told me she was expecting our first child. It was a City Deluxe and the bowl had burned right through. I kept the stem, though,' he added, after a moment of smoke-filled silence.

My own pipe was now lit, and I found that I didn't feel particularly anxious about whether it would *stay* lit. Pipe smokers en masse are no more intimidating or judgemental than they are individually.

I asked the assembly, 'What is the point of pipe smoking?'

Everyone smoked for a while and then Patrick Brain replied, 'It's a revolt against the speed of our daily life... Have you read *In Praise of Slow* by Carl Honoré?' I was about to ask whether Honoré talks about pipe smoking specifically in that book (he doesn't, I subsequently found out) when one of the pipemen interrupted, 'Somebody should send a copy to Gordon Brown!' and we were into the question of the public smoking ban, which deprives the current, depleted generation of British pipe smokers of what they see as their birthright: not so much the right to smoke in public places as the right to be detached. None of the previous generation of pipe smokers would have described themselves as being in 'revolt' against anything. 'It's intolerable,' said Patrick Brain, 'it's an assault on our civil liberties. His sentiments were echoed in between puffs of smoke from around the booth:

'It's health fascism...'

'It's obesity now...'

'And it'll be alcohol next...'

'You won't be able to smoke in your own home soon...'

'You already can't adopt children...'

The majority of the speakers considered pipes to be more or less harmless. 'Our problem,' drawled one of the members, 'is that what we do gets lumped in with *smoking*, meaning pernicious cigarette smoking. He said it used to be the case that you could put down 'non-smoker' on a life insurance application if you only smoked pipes. One man present had been weaned off cigarettes and on to pipes by his father, and he'd done the same with his own sons. He indicated two lads in their twenties, the youngest in the club by twenty years, who sat dutifully puffing away alongside him. It is held among many pipe smokers that 'the only danger is cancer of the mouth, which is very rare'.

I asked whether pipe smokers of today tended to be part of the libertarian right. This suggestion was digested during ten seconds of silent smoking before someone removed his pipe from his lips and said, 'Let's start a *real* row!' 'I think Che Guevara smoked a pipe, you know,' said Patrick Brain, 'and I know Bertrand Russell did.' (And then there's Tony Benn, Pipe Smoker of the Year 1992).

At length the pipes did their sedative work and the pipemen grew philosophical. There had been many previous assaults on Lady Nicotine, after all. Hadn't King James I tried to ban smoking for a while? We were now joined by one of several female members of the club, the marvellously named, and drolly engaging, Veda Lumber. She carried a couple of pipes in a leather case that I could see would have made the ideal gift for Uncle Sid: a Pipe Companion, it was called. I asked Veda how she came to start smoking pipes. 'I liked pipes and I liked tobacco,' she said, somewhat tautologically. 'You've got something left at the end of your smoke and you can watch it age. I was fifteen when I started. My father was a naval type, so he was okay about it. My mother thought it wasn't womanly.' But I suspect this was not a big consideration with Veda. She had worked as a schoolteacher and a prisoner custody officer. The group fell to reflecting on the unlikelihood of any criminal smoking a pipe. 'I don't know,' chuckled Patrick Brain, 'I'll bet Crippen did.' 'Didn't Albert Pierrepoint say he'd never hung a man who smoked a pipe?' someone else put in. That made sense, a pipe being a badge of honesty. 'The only criminal I know who did,' said Veda, 'was a fraudster.'

During my conversations in the backyard of the Thatcher's Arms, my pipe had gone out many times and I was stuck on a personal-best score of about twelve minutes. But I had been paying close attention to the pipe smokership of the club members. They'd puffed at varying speeds according to the state of the tobacco; they'd covered, or half-covered, the bowl with their fingers; and one of them had definitely *blown* down the stem in answer to some odd circumstance. I was thinking about all of this when parking my car in Mayfair one evening a couple of weeks later. I was feeling vaguely miserable and I had some time to kill; my pipe and tobacco were on the passenger seat of my car.

I would resort to the steadfast companionship of the briar. I loaded the pipe hastily, unselfconsciously, and somehow knew I was on to a winner as I introduced the first match. It immediately made a very promising glow in the bowl; the second match was hardly necessary. It was as though, after a period of wariness, my pipe had warmed to me.

At twenty past eight, I stepped out of my car and began to walk the streets of Mayfair. It was the first time I'd been at large in public with my pipe. I half expected to attract amused glances: *Such a young man to be smoking a pipe!* But I received no such glances. I looked, for better or for worse, a plausible pipeman, and I felt myself drawn to pipemen's places: Catholic churches, antiquarian bookshops. Passing one of the latter, I caught sight of my reflection – with pipe in mouth – in the window. It, or I, looked like the opening image of some hoary, but watchable, TV series: *Inspector Maigret Investigates.*

I walked on, and as I walked, I smoked, and kept *on* smoking. The church clocks of Mayfair chimed nine. I was smoking still, and it was not until about ten past that I resigned myself to the end of the pipe and tapped it on the top of a pillar box. All that came out was ash. I will never be Pipe Smoker of the Year, but I had become a pipe smoker, surely one of the last recruits to the brethren. ∎

CHINESE WHISPERS

Twenty years after Tiananmen Square, a journalist
puts her experiences under the microscope

Elizabeth Pisani

In April 1989, frustrated students from Beijing's elite universities
began squatting in Tiananmen Square. They had gathered there to
mourn the death of former Communist Party Chairman Hu Yaobang,
who had been pushed aside by the gerontocracy because of his
enthusiasm for political reform. What started as wreath-laying and
vague speech-making quickly swelled into open protest against the
hard-faced premier, Li Peng. In mid-May, the students ratcheted up
the drama with mass hunger strikes. Reinforcements streamed in from
the provinces and a rash of tents erupted across the symbolic heart of
the Chinese state.

From the centre of the chaos rose the Monument of the People's
Heroes, its terraces occupied by student leaders and foreign journalists.
Those on the north side of the monument looked into the steely eyes
of Chairman Mao Zedong, whose portrait surveyed the Square
from the Gate of Heavenly Peace, which bisects the city's main
thoroughfare, Chang'an jie, the Avenue of Eternal Peace. In front of
the Great Hall of the People on the western side of the Square was a

Students protesting during the hunger strike in Tiananmen Square, May 1989

makeshift medical centre for overzealous hunger strikers. On the other side, in front of the Museum of Chinese History, students from Hong Kong had set up a temporary canteen for non-strikers. It was grubby, haphazard, completely out of keeping with the intimidating majesty of the surrounding architecture, and it was a lot of fun. Students were escaping their overcrowded dorms, ignoring their time-serving lecturers, taking control of their lives and their country's future. They expressed themselves raucously through loudspeakers and sound systems that multiplied as the different groups grew more confident and began to squabble and fragment – those from Beijing elbowing each other around the monument, provincial students setting up headquarters in buses parked around the Square. They argued with one another as well as with a worker-run broadcast station and the government mouthpiece whose speakers were louder and clearer. It was a cacophony of democracy. But by the beginning of June, the law-and-order rhetoric pouring out of the government's loudspeakers was growing ever more uncompromising; patience was fraying and the city was growing sticky with tension.

I was a young reporter working for the Reuters news agency in Jakarta at the time. But as the protests dragged the small Beijing team deeper into exhaustion, the agency pulled in every Mandarin speaker they had. My degree in Chinese classics and history left me struggling for useful vocabulary, but it did at least provide some perspective. This was a Big Story on the daily news wires, but it was a Big Story in the sweep of Chinese history, too. I was ecstatic when I was sent first to cover the demonstrations in the southern city of Canton, then, at the end of May, to join the team in what we still called Peking. Realistic about my hubristic side and unimpressed by it, my editor sent me off with just one instruction: 'Remember, Elizabeth, a dead journalist is not a good journalist.'

So it was that Graham Earnshaw, then Reuters correspondent in Tokyo, and I spent the night of June 3–4 together in Tiananmen Square. In the letter of recommendation he wrote when I left Reuters, he said: 'On a more personal note, I'll never forget the night we spent together in Beijing.' And yet Graham and I remember it very differently. I discovered this about three years ago, when, scratching around on the Internet, I came across 'Graham Earnshaw's Memoirs', including an account of the events in Tiananmen Square that he had written in 2001. His narration was rich with the historical context and analysis you would expect of someone who has dedicated much of his life to decoding China, and full of the sharply observed detail of the talented journalist. And yet he had written me out of history, called into question the years of my dinner-party retellings of the events and undermined my faith in my own memory. I recall being in the Square when the tanks rolled in at dawn on June 4 to crush the demonstrations. In Graham's memory, I wasn't there.

I sulked for a couple of hours and then put it out of my mind. But now, with the twentieth anniversary of those events drawing near, I feel compelled to re-examine my memories. Ignoring decades of work by tens of thousands of neuroscientists, psychologists and philosophers, I thought I would run a very unscientific experiment, writing down as honestly as I can what I remember now about that night – the Late Record. Then I'll rummage around in my parents' basement in the hope of finding an account I wrote in 1989 – the Early Record. Then I'll trawl the Internet, hoping that Graham's memoirs, last seen three years ago, are still there – the Other Record. I'll lay the three memory outlines over each other like sheets of tracing paper to build up a map of that night. I'm interested most of all in the differences. Which facts and emotions did I lose? Have I found any new memories in the last two decades? Where, and why, are my memories different from those of my colleagues?

THE LATE RECORD, JANUARY 2009

Digging around in my memory, here's what I find: images that seem episodic, some in colour and pin-sharp, others in fuzzy black and white; scenes that don't flow naturally, edited together in my mind.

Memories of June 3 begin some time in the early afternoon, when the sun grew hot and the Square was hung about with a stench that smeared itself on the back of the throat and stuck there. I was hungry. Well-funded American television stations had organized relays of beer and sandwiches for their crews on the front line but Reuters didn't stretch to deliveries. As big-boned South Africans swapped stories from war zones, downed the beer and swung their TV cameras about, I watched students stubbing out cigarettes and collapsing into a groaning heap in anticipation of the lens. Occasionally I translated their groans and suffering: 'I was beaten by a soldier who was crazed on drugs' – this from a broken boy who not five minutes before had been energetically triumphant in a card game. But I still hadn't been offered a sandwich.

The competing broadcasts were relentless. Many described a stand-off between troops and indignant citizens on the outskirts of the city, some raked over rumours of army insurrections and imminent assault. But in the fetid afternoon air there didn't seem much to be afraid of. Or rather, I don't remember being afraid. I passed my time interviewing student leaders.

'What is it you're really fighting for?'

'Democracy.'

'Okay, but what do you mean by democracy?'

'Freedom.'

'And how would you characterize freedom?'

'Democracy.'

Perhaps the subtleties of the argument were hidden by the thick regional accents: many of the Beijing-based students had drifted back to campus to sit their exams. Democracy and/or freedom are all very well, but one found that, beneath their idealism, many of the kids at the top universities understood that job qualifications were a better bet.

Reuters had an antediluvian mobile phone, nicknamed 'the brick', but the network was unreliable and the battery life brief. I'd been hoarding coins since my arrival in China, and that afternoon I scoped out the payphones around the Square, just in case. I was also looking for a modicum of privacy. Those war-bitten cameramen thought they'd seen it all, but none of them had ever had to change a Tampax in a revolution. Odd that my memories of that afternoon are so physical – the hunger, the bodily functions, the exhaustion. I was longing to lie down: I had that dry-behind-the-eyeballs feeling of the extremely sleep-deprived, as if a bare light bulb had been left on in my head and I couldn't switch it off. But I must have had an hour or two's sleep that morning, because I remember worrying, when I woke up, that my dreams of gunfire, beatings and troop movements would merge with my memory and creep into my reporting.

Then there's a blank; the image comes into focus again at nightfall. It is of a Reuters photographer hanging on a ladder in front of a public building – was it the history museum? – aiming his camera at angry crowds who were hurling stones and insults at blank-faced soldiers. A commander came out of the building and yelled at the crowds, yelled at the great blond photographer on his ladder. I yelled at him too. A dead photographer is not a good photographer. As the hysteria mounted, so did the volume on the warring loudspeakers. The government ordered everyone home. The students reported that troops were storming the barricades that the people of Beijing had erected at the main entry points to the city centre. Tanks were on the move and bullets were flying. Troop reinforcements were arriving at the railway station, they said.

I got on my bike and headed east along Chang'an jie towards the station. Beijing is a city that was designed to make people feel small in the face of the Emperor, its broad avenues marching straight ahead before lines of glowering public buildings. The avenue that led to the train station, just south of Jianguo Men (the Gate of National Sovereignty), was carpeted with soldiers, country boys with ringworm showing through their crew cuts, sitting on the ground in silence, waiting for something to happen.

Troops in the heart of Beijing. This was news, as far as I knew. I looked for a phone. Then somehow I was looking out at the soldiers from an empty Korean restaurant. I was attended by heavily painted working girls who let me use the phone, solved my personal hygiene dilemma and wouldn't let me go until I was fortified by noodles and kimchi.

· I cycled back the way I had come but the Avenue of Eternal Peace had turned into what seemed like a war zone, invaded by heavy green tanks rumbling westwards towards the Square. I dashed into the Jianguo Hotel and called the Reuters bureau again.

'Tanks headed for the Square.'

A pause. 'Are you sure they're tanks?'

'Of course I'm sure, big green things, heavy, metal.'

'Not APCs?'

What's an APC? I thought. I usually report on badminton tournaments and the Jakarta stock market, goddamit.

A sigh. 'Wheels or treads?'

I ran out – wheels – ran back, redialled.

'That would be an armoured personnel carrier then. Do try to be accurate, Elizabeth.'

I returned to the Square. At the monument I found a clutch of journalists, including Graham, whose Chinese was far better than mine. I was glad to see him there. We looked out over the Square. Most of the canvas tents had been abandoned, most of the students who were still around were gathered up on the monument. The broadcasts continued: news of troop movements around the city, inspirational addresses from Hou Dejian, a Taiwanese pop star who was trying to revive the students' flagging spirits by squatting in the Square himself, taking on the hunger strike that the masses had already abandoned.

Suddenly, loud bangs and dotted arcs of fire rained into the Square: tracer bullets, designed to illuminate the target for heavier artillery and/or to scare the enemy. I remember thinking, God, those are beautiful, and Oh shit, this is for real, almost as one thought. The hardbitten camera crews picked up their tripods and left with as much bravado as they could muster: 'Got to protect the equipment.' Graham and I looked at each other. We weren't hotshot correspondents flown in from Jo'burg or Beirut or New York to cover yet another more or less interchangeable conflict. We were here because we'd studied Chinese history. Now we had a chance to witness it and we weren't going to give it up.

The last time we managed to get through to the office on the brick, our colleagues sounded nervous. A dead journalist is not a good journalist, but an editor who allows journalists to die is more or less a dead editor. The desk told us that we should leave, because our colleague, Andy Roche, was on the other side of the Square, 'phoning in all the same stuff'. I learned later that they told Andy he should leave because we were the other side of the Square, 'phoning in all the same stuff'. Shortly after that call Andy was arrested by thugs from military intelligence, badly beaten and dumped in a suburb. Perhaps the thugs knew what was about to happen and wanted to minimize witnesses. Perhaps Andy was just in the wrong place at the wrong time. Unaware of this, Graham and I remained stubborn. And we remained in the Square.

June 3 melted into June 4, but still it was dark. Tiananmen Square covers a hundred acres. From the monument, it was hard for us to see what was going on under Chairman Mao's nose at the north end, where the Avenue of Eternal Peace passes the portrait of Mao. But at a certain point – when, I have no idea – we became aware that troops were massing up there. We made our way across to the east of the Square, in front of the history museum. Graham was limping – I didn't know whether from an injury or a childhood illness. Time passed and he broke out his stores: a can of Pepsi and a mint Aero bar, generously shared with me. Green chocolate. I inhaled it at the time. I've never been able to stomach it since.

At dawn, one of the student broadcast stations crackled back into life. It was Hou Dejian, the Taiwanese pop star. He'd taken it upon himself to go and negotiate with the general in charge of the troops at the north of the Square and he reported that they'd done a deal. The army would give the students until seven a.m. to clear out of the Square. After that, tanks would roll in and crush everything and everyone they found there.

'Since it's a democracy movement, we should take a vote,' the singer yelled. 'Should we stay or should we go?' From where I stood it sounded like a dead heat, but Hou, self-appointed arbiter of democracy, declared that the 'Go's' had it and said that the military had asked everyone to leave by the south-east corner of the Square. The motley group of students who had stuck out the confusion, the fear, the hunger, the stench – a few hundred, I'd say – hauled themselves wearily to their feet and started to head for safety.

It was an extraordinary moment, and a great story – the only time in history I could think of when a challenge to central authority in China had been dismissed without violence. And, of course, our phone was dead. Because I'd mapped out the public phones and because I was quicker on my feet, we decided that I should run and file the story, while Graham witnessed the rest of the withdrawal. I ran past the front of the museum and dived into an alleyway just off the Square, but the payphone cord had been cut. I couldn't find my bike, so I took someone else's and set off northwards, sticking to the east side of the Square and heading for Chang'an jie. One part of my brain was writing the lead to the biggest story of my career so far: 'Taiwanese pop star negotiates peaceful end to student demonstrations'. And, with another part of my brain: 'Those are APCs rolling towards me, not tanks. Do try to be accurate, Elizabeth.' It was about five in the morning.

There were two other civilians on foot ahead of me going in the same direction. It wasn't until the second one crumpled before my eyes, a blow-up doll deflated by a bullet from a figure who'd popped out of a hatch in the APC closest to us, that my brain put the two parts of the picture together and realized that they didn't match. I turned tail and pedalled furiously back down the side of the Square to Graham. I still have the image in my mind of a kid in a white coat, a medical student, who was scooping a fallen body up on to the flatbed of a transport tricycle. I seem to remember a white hatchback with a red cross on it and the incongruous words: GIFT FROM THE PEOPLE OF ITALY. I saw a tank, definitely a tank, roll over a pack of bicycles, and found myself worrying that mine might be in the mangle. I worried, too, about Graham, who couldn't run very fast, who needed somewhere safe to wait out the chaos.

He was still where I'd left him, on the side of the Square close to the history museum. We set off together down another side alley, this time to the south-east. More dead payphones. Much chaos. A family had opened the gates to a compound and they let Graham in, grudgingly.

I had to file the story, but I also had my editor sitting on my shoulder whispering 'dead is not good'. Although I hadn't used it yet, I knew Reuters had a room on the fourth floor of the nearby Peking Hotel for journalists to rest in on breaks between reporting. That would be safe and my colleague James Kynge, who had been reporting for several days straight and had been given the room for the night, might have a phone that worked. But the hotel was the other side of Chang'an jie, and the Avenue of Eternal Peace was less peaceful than ever, with wave after wave of tanks progressing westwards down it towards the north of the Square. In my memory, I dashed across the line of fire in order to file the story. Though perhaps that came with the retelling. Perhaps, actually, I slunk through one of the many urine-puddled underpasses where, in quieter times, moon-faced Uighur boys shook down backpackers for dollars. I simply can't be sure.

Now, another clear, polished bit. When I got to the Peking Hotel I found the front door barred, a line of soldiers standing wide-legged behind the locked glass. No one was getting in or out.

Then came the memory of a long, lazy summer in my backpacking years. An American spy whom I had met on a train platform in the furthest reaches of western China had lent me a room in the Peking Hotel; an unutterable luxury compared with the fleapits of my travels. On another train platform, further east in Xi'an, I'd met a pretty American boy. We shared a bunk on the train to Beijing where he was shoe-horned into an overcrowded student dorm. When the spy was called away, it seemed a shame not to have the pretty boy share my luxurious quarters. On the other hand, I didn't want to abuse the spy's hospitality by being indiscreet. So it was that I learned about the side entrances to the Peking Hotel, the ones used by the delivery boys and engineers. Now, with tanks rolling along the avenue behind me, I felt my way back to one of those service doors and was in.

I went straight for the bank of payphones on the ground floor. All dead. I headed for the Reuters room, but when the lift doors opened on the fourth floor, they opened on to a construction site. I must have looked absolutely devastated because someone else in the lift, from his haircut and dress an overseas Chinese, asked if he could help. 'A phone. I need a phone.'

He took me to a room on one of the highest floors and knocked an 'it's only me' rat-tat-tat code. The door opened, but there was nobody there. Then I looked down. The room was crowded, but everyone was snaking around on the floor on their bellies, fearful that a stray bullet might make it up seven floors, through the concrete balcony and double-glazed window and into the room.

My stomach wobbled as I picked up the phone. Miraculously, it was working. I called the Reuters bureau and my words tripped over one another in the rush to be heard. After a sentence, 'Hold on.' Click, the newsflash hit the world: CHINESE TROOPS ENTER SQUARE, FIRE ON STUDENTS.

'Go.'

More racing, stumbling, tripping.

'Hold on.'

Tap, tap, tap, click. That was the newsbreak, the one-sentence lead. I drew breath. 'Go.'

I told of the pop star, the negotiation, the promise, the betrayal. Paragraph by paragraph my fractured account was woven together by my colleague Bob Basler, hitting the news wires in flawless prose.

When I ran dry, 'Good. Are you okay?' I gave news of Graham and was told to join James in the Reuters room. It was indeed on the fourth floor of the Peking Hotel but in the old block; I had gone to the new, high-rise tower by mistake. As I left, the Hong Kong journalists were off their bellies and fighting for the phone, so that they could phone in their own 'eyewitness accounts' to their editors.

What else do I remember from that time? Crawling around the

rooftop of the Peking Hotel with James later that day and the next, trying for a bird's-eye view of the Square (we could see the final barricade, but no one could see into the Square itself). Phoning in every microscopic troop movement, until the desk cracked with boredom and pleaded with us to stop. Watching the citizens of Beijing surge forward on to the barricades, taunting the teenage soldiers and calling them names until they, too, cracked. They would leap up from their seated ranks and charge towards the barricades, firing the occasional shot, mowing down the odd enraged citizen. Then they would turn and saunter back to their spot. On one occasion, a soldier wheeled around a second time, casually picking off a figure who had rushed forward to claim a fallen body. For some reason this upset me more than anything else I saw.

I can visualize the image of a naked body strung up by the neck, hanging from a burnt-out tank in broad daylight. The tank is facing west, the body hanging from its south side, Mao's portrait to the north. Flies buzzing. A smell. But can I have seen that, heard it, smelled it? Not before June 4, surely, because I wasn't aware of any deaths before then. And not after, because we couldn't get near enough the Square to have a fix on Mao's portrait.

I remember, a day or two later, walking north-east across Beijing to get back to the office in San Li Tun, an area that was then dominated by diplomats and has now been overrun by thumping music bars. Even before I'd left, my colleagues had gone into boy mode, stacking up on soft drinks and chocolate. I was pretty sure they'd be in need of something healthier and stopped at the market. I bought heaps of strawberries, apricots and lettuce. When I got to the office I gave these to the cleaning ladies to wash. There was a sharp intake of breath. The cleaning ladies worked for the Chinese intelligence services; they weren't expected to do any actual cleaning. But having been asked, they had to play their roles.

When I sat down to read the wires, I saw that we had just filed a story about the city being strangled into starvation because no food could reach the markets. Later, when the Reuters staff magazine asked for a photo of me in action reporting the crisis, the only shot I could find was one of me holding plates of strawberries and apricots. What a hero!

THE EARLY RECORD V. THE LATE RECORD (WITH INTERVENTIONS FROM THE OTHER RECORD)

My basement excavations have led me to a folder containing thirteen yellowing handwritten pages, titled 'A Summer's Morning in Beijing'. It's an account that I wrote in 1989, perhaps because I feared exactly the sort of forgetting that is with me now. I can't remember when I wrote it; some time after the twenty-four-hour window in which most experiences get written from our short- to our long-term memories, certainly, but no more than a few weeks after the 'unforgettable night'. And on the Web, I've found Graham's account. Having committed the Late Record to paper, sitting down to read my early account and Graham's makes me feel slightly sick, as if I'm about to exhume a dead body.

The Early Record, written in 1989, agrees with the Late Record in recounting exhaustion, hunger, Tampax, mint Aero and the dinner provided by Korean hookers. All the physical stuff, strongly felt but tied very loosely to specific times or places. Encouragingly, the Early Record also agrees with Graham's account on virtually everything that we witnessed together until, with no explanation, he pushes the button on me and makes me evaporate:

> I stayed. I moved at some point over to the kerb on the side of the Square, under the trees. The students remaining had grouped themselves around the Monument. Elizabeth left and went back to the Peking Hotel to get word of what was happening on the Square through to Reuters office and the world...

Graham airbrushes out any possibility that I could have travelled up towards the troops, watched them roll towards me, witnessed a civilian shot just a few metres in front of me, because he has me gone long before dawn. With the loss of my place in the Square that morning

I also lose an important part of my sense of self, someone who, just once, witnessed history.

From the Early Record, I can now see that over the last twenty years, I've run a couple of days together. I wasn't even in the Square on the afternoon of June 3, the time I remember spending scoping out payphones, translating student soap operas for the cameramen, feeling nauseous in the thickening smell of a warm afternoon. Those things must have happened the day before, because I spent that afternoon in the Reuters office, trying to make myself useful and waiting for my shift in the Square, which didn't start until close to dusk.

That's when the accounts start to agree again, around the time things are getting ugly and the photographer is setting himself up on his ladder. It wasn't at the history museum that the students began to hurl stones, but at the back of the Great Hall of the People, which lies on the other side of the Square. The Early Record describes the attack on the hall in some detail. Though I have climbed a tree for a better view, the photographer on the ladder doesn't appear. Here's what I wrote:

> Workers are lobbing rocks, smashing those fancy streetlamps inside the compound, ripping up the railings and using them to smash up paving stones for ammo… Occasionally, a lobby of stones will come back the other way… At one stage [the workers] force the gate open but stop on the threshold, as if suddenly aware that they are at the Point of No Return. They politely close the gates again, and continue to hurl stones.

The ugliness was, it seems, localized. In the vastness of the Square I go on to find friendly exchanges between soldiers, citizens and students, swaps of cigarettes and water, orchestrated singing of patriotic songs by all and sundry. Things are relaxed enough for me to go off with another reporter, United Press International's Jonathan Landay, to find food.

> Miserably unsuccessful, but we kill a couple of cold beers and talk about the hopelessness of keeping a marriage/relationship intact in this absurd business.

I did cycle towards the train station, as I now remember, and I did find soldiers with guns. But the scene was less tense than I now recall. At the time I found them 'sitting on the road. Some are smoking, some are lying down in the laps of others...'

I describe people handing their kids up to sit on soldiers' laps, citizens exchanging cigarettes for a look at their semi-automatic weapons. I do duck into a Korean girlie bar to use the phone, calling in a report of heavily armed troops in central Beijing, but even as I do I talk of the 'general friendliness of the scene'.

Two decades of polishing the story of my night of terror in Beijing has worn away the relaxed moments, the cold beers and suburban gossip, the companionable stand-off that persisted until close to midnight. Is that because aggression makes for a better story, and makes me a braver witness, a more dedicated journalist? Or has my memory been remade in the image of history's judgement? Have I rubbed out all the bits that don't fit with the narrative that we seem collectively to have agreed on: a nakedly aggressive military machinery bent on crushing democratic aspirations at any price?

I'm relieved that, although some details differ, on the major points of history all three accounts agree: the camera crews left early 'to protect the equipment' and when the remaining journalists decided to leave once the troops started massing, Graham and I stayed. And though Graham then sends me away, his own account also contains the peace deal brokered by the pop star, the vote, the exodus. My Early and Late Records agree on my journey northwards across the Square in search of a phone, although I was apparently on foot and not on a bike. They agree on the troops coming down the Square towards me, on the two other civilians stumbling towards the troops ahead of me:

> The one furthest in front (about 10 metres from me) gets set upon by foot soldiers who have these big rubber whip things. The top to the nearest APC pops open, a couple of shots dance around the three of us and the second chap, about 5 metres in front of me, goes down. I turn tail. By the time I am level with the history museum the med students are loading limp bodies on to makeshift stretchers

and into ambulances. For the 15 minutes that I am around after this, the stream of bodies, stretchers, ambulances is more or less constant. At a distance of even a metre it is hard to tell an unconscious body from a corpse, and I cannot swear before my heart that several dozen people died on the Square. I can and did save my only tears for the inevitable moment when official television announced: 'not a single person died in Tiananmen Square'.

Memory is abstract, personal, unknowable. It can encompass the random and the inexplicable, just as dream sequences can. But once memories are written down, or otherwise committed to the record, they assume a life of their own. They become less malleable and must assume a more coherent shape. We take fragments of memory and weave them together into patterns as best we can. We darn or embroider any holes with threads of things that happened in our readings, in our conversations with others who really were there, in our dreams. Those then become part of the fabric of our storytelling, so that soon enough it is impossible to say what was remembered and what was embroidered. They become our memories, in the way that the soldier's blackened body hanging from a tank has become part of my memory. Here's what Graham says about that incident:

> The Reuters photographers had some extraordinary pictures, including stuff shot by a totally crazy American cowboy who gloried in the named of Rambo – a tall, lanky guy with bleached blond hair who took the most insane risks... His most memorable photo for me was of a PLA soldier hanging from a bus at the Xidan intersection on Changan Avenue to the west of Tiananmen Square. The soldier's body was burnt to a crisp. It was disgusting, and it was decided not to send it to subscribers.

I'm now convinced I saw the photo, not the reality, but at least my memory about a blond photographer up a ladder making a target of himself now makes sense.

We need stories to impose order on events and emotions that would otherwise seem disjointed. When I'd called the Reuters bureau close to midnight and remarked on the 'general friendliness of the scene', Bob Basler had replied, 'Well it's not so friendly where Guy is [Guy Dinmore was Reuters Bureau Chief in Beijing]. They're killing people in the west of town.' There were hundreds of foreign journalists in Beijing that night, and tens of thousands of citizens on the streets. Many witnessed some form of shooting, saw bodies fall, watched blood pools spreading. Most of the journalists were also sleep-deprived, thirsty, frightened, needing to pee or eat; many were confused by a cacophony of orders, exhortations, pleadings in a language they didn't speak. And each one of us could only observe a tiny corner of a story that would be one of the biggest of our lives. In those circumstances, to say 'I've no idea what's going on' just won't do.

Foreigners with a special interest in China know that 'the Tiananmen massacre' acts as a convenient shorthand for a much messier and certainly very bloody reality that affected the whole of Beijing. But for many other people outside China, the narrative has been rewritten around that single geographical point. For many people in China, of course, there's no narrative at all. The events of that night have been wiped from the record entirely. So much so that three editors on a provincial newspaper were sacked in 2007 because a young clerk, clueless about what had happened eighteen years before, allowed a tribute to the victims of '4/6' to slip into the classified ads column.

Journalism, it is said, is the first draft of history. But this first draft is edited before it even hits the page, or the airwaves, by individual journalists who weave facts into a story that will engage the reader. It then gets edited over time into the dominant narrative. Details that seemed important to a reporter in the moment – friendly troops, babies on laps – get drowned by larger events and eventually disappear.

But whether or not we are honest about it, the knowledge that our journalism shapes our personal narratives affects what we report at least as much as the hunger, fear, exhaustion and hubris that occupy large parts of our minds in a war zone. While we pretend to ourselves that we are neutral observers, simply recording events as we see them, we all want to be at the centre of the stories we tell.

I have never doubted that I left the Square with Graham. When I found my 1989 account of events, here is what it said:

> I explained that we needed a phone, and a kid volunteered to take me on his bike. We thought it best, at that point, to leave the Square together and so followed this kid... around into that alley with the restaurant that was never open when I was hungry... Finally, the kid offered us the bike. 'Just take it.' Graham looked agitated as I tried to swing my crotch over a crossbar that would have been a better fit for my armpit. Wobbled, crashed, tried again, wobbled again, but this time in the direction of the Beijing Fandian [Peking Hotel].

This was of no conceivable historical importance. In the second draft of history this little description would certainly be on the editor's spike. So why did I feel the need to record it in such detail, two decades ago, and why do I seize on it now? Because my presence in Tiananmen Square when the troops started moving across it is fundamental to my identity. It's of no importance to Graham, of course. His memory doesn't have to hold on to my wobbling away on a bike. I hold on to Graham in my memory perhaps because it allows me to play the hero. In the Late Record I made sure he was taken by a family into a compound, that he was safe, before going off to file the story. In fact, I left Graham standing in an alleyway. In any case, he was demonstrably in no need of help from me, but my imagined act of altruism has been much rehearsed in subsequent retellings.

Neither the Early Record nor the Late Record finds me afraid. This is surprising because at the time, I was apparently contemplating death. I don't remember these thoughts now, but in 1989 I recorded them in the purple prose of the twenty-four-year-old:

> The air is light with the intoxicating fumes of impending martyrdom. I think these kids, like me, are protected by the arrogance of youth from contemplating anything so dusty as death... Better to have someone else weeping for the life we might have led than to have to do it ourselves after decades of smudged dreams.

Just now, when I came to write the Late Record, I couldn't actually recall the thumping in the chest and clenching of the genitals that say: I'm scared. And yet I'm aware that fear hangs heavy over dinner-table retellings. Confessing that I was afraid makes me seem at once braver (I hung in there despite my fear) and more human (I'm not ashamed to admit my vulnerability, even in a world where everyone drinks testosterone for breakfast). Saying I was terrified makes for a better story. It also makes me a liar.

I am the sum of my experiences, but does that mean the events and emotions that I lived through, or the sum of my experiences as I now remember them, grow muscular, honed and polished with years of retelling? Can I claim as my own the feelings, images, thoughts that I have sucked back in from the collective memory? Do I become a different person as my memory changes, or do I change my memories because I am becoming a different person?

Like Graham, I will never forget the night we spent in Beijing. But I'm resigned to the fact that the landscapes of memory shift constantly. We can overlay as many records as we like, but we'll never tell the same story twice. ∎

CENSORED
Bruce Connew

Last spring, on my way back to New Zealand from Dubrovnik, I stopped over in Hong Kong and took a ferry from the airport, up the Pearl River Delta to Zhongshan, a small (by Chinese standards), agreeable city in Guangdong province. It was friends of friends in Zhongshan who loaned me their subscription copy of *National Geographic*, a special, pre-Olympic Games issue on China, which I had returned after a few days. I decided to buy a copy of my own. I found one in Zhongshan's chief bookstore, upstairs in Holiday Plaza. It appeared to be the only English-language magazine in a well-stocked shop. It was sealed in polythene.

Back at my hotel, I took off the wrapping and started to flip through it. On page forty-six, I stopped. Two and a bit lines on the left-hand page had been crossed out in heavy black ink. Censored, I deduced – it was not long until the Olympic Games. Everywhere else in the world people were discussing whether the Games would provoke change in the Chinese government, but China is China.

And this was *National Geographic*. Why would any government want to censor such a normally uncontroversial magazine, even the Chinese government? It was true, however, that when I tilted the page, I could just make out what was underneath the black ink: '...the Japanese invasion to the Cultural Revolution to the massacre around Tiananmen Square in 1989'. So this was an unusually provocative piece for *National Geographic*.

I carried on, and soon came to a page that felt thicker and stiffer than the others. At first I assumed it was a three-page foldout, but then I realized that two pages had been completely glued together. Further on, I found two more double-page spreads that were glued together and spent nearly an hour carefully prising them apart. They had been stuck around the red border of each page, which might have been made for the task. Then the censor had twice drawn his or her glue-stick diagonally across the page in a neat, symbolic cross that, when I tried to peel the pages apart, tore at the ink, ensuring whatever had been written there was lost forever and immortalizing the censor's work.

I examined what lay beneath. On one spread, under the headline MINORITIES, was a map of China with each minority assigned its own colour: the problem must have been that Taiwan, which China claims as part of its territory, was colourless. A second spread, 'Mao Now', showed four works by Chinese artists, each depicting Mao. One of these, Gao Qiang's 'Swimming Mao', according to *National Geographic,* 'was banned'. A third spread, with the title 'Cutting Off Dissent', presented a full-page artwork by Sheng Qi – a photograph of his left hand cradling a 'boyhood' photograph, which showed his missing little finger, which he had cut off in protest at the Tiananmen Square massacre in 1989.

Had the censor been in China, or in America? The magazine was turning out to be a collector's item. I admit: I returned to the bookstore and bought another copy in its polythene wrapper, which remains sealed. Back home, I made a few enquiries. I found only one reference online, but it proved I wasn't the only person to have bought a censored copy. At *National Geographic,* the director of media relations confirmed what I pretty much knew: 'someone connected with local magazine distribution in Asia glued together a few pages of the May 2008 issue'. It was an isolated incident, and there had been no official or unofficial communication about it. 'It does happen occasionally in some countries that distributors feel they need to take local sensibility into account.' It was a hazard of global sales.

Mulling over the layers of art and politics involved, I realized I had unwittingly prepared an artwork of my own, right there in the Louis Hotel. I had three of the spreads photographed to produce a political triptych (*Censored* 2008), three large pigment prints each twice the size of a *National Geographic* double-page spread; my personal recontextualization of these pages. ∎

CUTTING OFF DISSENT

Something vital is missing in China. Yet its absence is still felt, raising a question that lingers like a phantom limb: Can the ruling Communist Party continue to suppress political dissent among one-fifth of the world's population? While China has embraced economic development, it remains a repressive one-party state. Monitoring newspapers, magazines, artwork, and more, government functionaries regularly detain citizens whose ideas might undermine China's constitutionally enshrined values of "security, honor, and interests of the motherland." The party's Publicity Department (formerly the Propaganda Department) sends daily directives to journalists on how to cover the "news." And while the Internet is a conduit for information, it also serves as a surveillance tool for the party, which slaps dissidents with demotion, dismissal, or imprisonment. Last year 29 members of the press spent China's National Journalists' Day behind bars. Foreign reporters feel the pinch too. Says one: "The aim is intimidation and fear, and it works." In a recent assessment of press freedom by Reporters Without Borders, China ranked 163 out of 169 nations. Some pundits say censorship will inevitably disappear as countries "engage" China, but others say that's far too optimistic. As James Mann, author of *The China Fantasy: Why Capitalism Will Not Bring Democracy to China*, observes, "As other authoritarian leaders around the world seek to stifle political opposition, they look to China as a model." —*Alan Mairson*

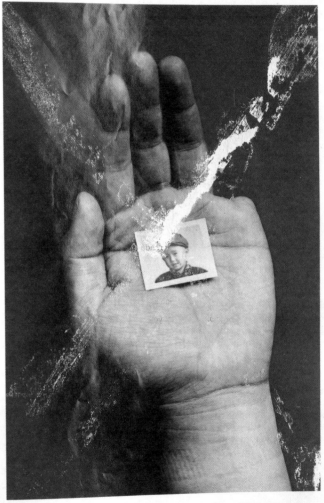

To protest the events of Tiananmen Square in 1989, artist Sheng Qi cut off his finger. He created a series of photographs of his hand, in this one holding a boyhood photo.

Chinese history has become the story of average citizens. But there are risks when a nation depends on the individual dreams of 1.3 billion people rather than a coherent political system with clear rule of law.

Occasionally the old anger flared up, like the massive demonstrations that followed NATO's bombing of the Chinese Embassy in Belgrade in 1999. That same year, protests by Falun Gong practitioners made headlines; a few years later the outbreak of SARS briefly occupied the world's attention.

But these incidents were most remarkable for how little they affected the lives of average Chinese. It was different from the narrative of the 20th century: After 1900, when the Boxer Rebellion swept across Beijing, every decade included at least one major political upheaval. Usually these events were violent, ranging from ▓▓▓▓▓▓▓▓▓▓▓▓▓▓▓▓▓▓▓▓▓▓▓ ▓▓▓▓▓ Together they made for a troubled century, which was why my students wrote so delicately about the past.

Perhaps this awareness of a painful history was also why the 1990s turned out differently. It became modern China's first decade without a major upheaval, and thus far the 21st century has also been peaceful. And yet despite the lack of political change, the nation has been radically transformed. For three decades the economy has grown at an average annual rate of nearly 10 percent, and more people have been lifted out of poverty than in any other country, at any other time. China has become home to the largest urbanization in human history—an estimated 150 million people have left the countryside, mostly to work in the factory towns of the coast. By most measures the nation is now the world's largest consumer, using more grain, meat, coal, and steel than the United States. But apart from

Deng Xiaoping, it's difficult to credit these critical changes to any specific government official. The Communist Party's main strategy has been to unleash the energy of the people, at least in the economic sense. In today's China, government is decentralized, and people can freely start businesses, find new jobs, move to new homes. After a century of powerful leaders and political turmoil, Chinese history has become the story of average citizens.

But there are risks when a nation depends on the individual dreams of 1.3 billion people rather than a coherent political system with clear rule of law. China faces an environmental crisis—the nation has become the world's leading emitter of carbon dioxide, and there's a serious shortage of water and other basic resources. The gap between rich and poor has become dangerously wide. The difference between urban and rural incomes is greater than three to one—the largest since the reforms began in 1978. Each of these problems is far too broad to be solved, or even grasped, by the average citizen. And because the government continues to severely restrict political freedom, people are accustomed to avoiding such issues. My students taught me that everything was personal—history, politics, foreign relations—but this approach creates boundaries as well as connections. For many Chinese, if a problem doesn't affect them personally, it might as well not exist.

Over the years I've stayed in touch with more than one hundred of my former students. The cheap onionskin paper is long gone; today they communicate by email and cell phone. Most are still teaching, and they live in small cities—part of the new middle class. Because of migration, their old villages are dying, like rural regions all across China. "Only old people and small children are left at home," a woman named Maggie recently wrote. "It seems that the countryside now is under Japanese attacks, all the people have fled."

Although my students were patient with the flaws of their elders, today they seem to feel a greater distance from the young people they teach. "When we were students there wasn't a generation gap with the teachers," wrote Sally. "Nowadays our students have their own viewpoints and ideas, and they speak about democracy and freedom, independence and rights. I think we fear them instead of them fearing us." A classmate pointed out that most of today's students come from one-child homes, and many have been spoiled by indulgent parents. "We had a pure childhood," wrote Lucy. "But now the students are different, they are more influenced by modern things, even sex. But when we were young, sex was a tatoo for us."

Recently I sent out a short questionnaire asking how their lives have changed. Responses came from across the country, ranging from Zhejiang Province on the east coast to Tibet in the far west. Most described their material lives as radically different. "When I graduated in 1998, I told my Mum, if I got 600 yuan [about $70] each month, I would be satisfied," Roger wrote. "In fact I got 400 yuan then, and now each month I get about 1700 yuan." When I asked about their most valuable possession, 70 percent said that they had bought an apartment, usually with loans. One had recently purchased a car. They were still optimistic. When I asked them to rate their feelings about the future on a scale of one to ten, with ten being the most positive, the average response was 6.5.

I asked what worried them the most. Several mentioned relationships; one woman wrote: "The marriage is not safe any more in China, it is more common for people around here to break up." A couple of respondents who now work far from home were concerned about their status as migrants. "I am like a foreigner in China," Willy

wrote. But the most common source of worry seemed to be mortgage payments. "Ten years ago, I worried that I could not have a good and warm family," Belinda wrote. "Now I am worried about my loan at the bank." None of her classmates expressed concern about political reform, foreign relations, or any other national issue. Nobody mentioned the environment.

FOR YEARS I didn't hear from Vanessa. Finally, half a decade after I had taught her, I received an email. She had found a sales position with a company that produced electronic components: "I am changed a lot. I am in Shenzhen now, which is a big city in China.... Do you know American companies like America II or Classic components corp? They are our customers. I am little proud to have opportunity to co-operate with them. Because they are very big companies in the world, President Bush even visited America II last year. And the big reason I like my work now is I can use my language I learned."

The next time I was in Shenzhen, we met in the lobby of the Shangri-La Hotel. "Did you see my car?" Vanessa said, and then she looked disappointed that I had missed her arrival. She explained that her fiancé had just given her the vehicle as a gift. "He's the boss of my company," she said.

She was still quite pretty, and I couldn't help but conjure a stereotypical boss image: a leering man in his 50s, smoking Chunghwa cigarettes and shouting into a cell phone. But I said I'd like to meet him.

"Oh, he's waiting," Vanessa said. "He had to drive, because I don't have my license yet. I've been too busy!"

We walked outside. In the parking lot sat a silver BMW Z4 3.0i convertible coupe—in China, a hundred-thousand-dollar car. I peered inside: no cigarettes, no cell phone. Crew cut, acne, rumpled clothes. He smiled politely, stepped out of the car, and shook my hand. The company boss was all of 27 years old.

▶ **Behind the Pictures** Photographer Fritz Hoffmann shares stories about his images at **ngm.com**.

MAO NOW

H.I.A.C.S.

Surely Mao must be spinning in his crystal coffin. The founder of the People's Republic of China, who decreed "there is no such thing as art for art's sake," has himself become an objet d'art. As attention shifts from making revolution to making money, and intellectuals debate Mao's legacy as hero or villain, artists cash in on politically charged, tongue-in-cheek (and flower-on-cheek) versions of the Buddha-like face. Some images are too charged: Gao Qiang's "Swimming Mao" was banned. "The government was unable to undergo the moral test," Gao says. Even before he became the darling of art galleries, Mao had been crowned the king of kitsch; his image decorates T-shirts and watches. The great leap forward from Red Guard to avant-garde probably began with Andy Warhol's 1972 silk screen portraits; one just sold for 17.4 million dollars to, fittingly, a Hong Kong tycoon. Call it the ultimate Chinese brand. —Cathy Newman

The many faces of Mao, from far left: Mao with a Stalinesque mustache; swimming in a blood-red Yangtze River; flower-cheeked; and out of focus.

Evangelical Christians spread the word in Southend-on-Sea, 1974

IF WITH HIS SKIRT HE DO TOUCH BREAD OR POTTAGE

Don Paterson

The 'Baldragon' in Baldragon Academy means something like 'farm of the warrior', and is disappointingly unrelated either to Baal or to dragons. Nonetheless, in the mid-Seventies it did its bit to live up to its folk etymology, and for new arrivals from the gentler primary schools of Macalpine and Downfield it was an unimaginable hellhole. Not that we hadn't *tried* to imagine it: but despite reassurances from our mothers that the horror stories were merely big boys' tales meant to put the wind up us, everything turned out to be true, and worse.

Baldragon had recently been merged – I swear I'm not making this up – with the local borstal, on the reasonable grounds that the bad boys' transition into mainstream education would be smoother here than anywhere else. Baldragon was a rough school long before their arrival, though – one where the children would ease their frustration by hurling chairs through closed windows or ripping the legs off pigeons, and teachers would ease theirs by belting children insensible with a vinegar-soaked leather tawse. One enterprising art teacher liked to place the child inside a dark cupboard with his arm sticking through the door and his hand out, so the kid had no idea when the strap would fall. We heard talk of various awareness-raising exercises designed to train staff out of their old habits, but we would've settled for a vague request to observe the Geneva Convention. And war it was. 'Granny' Gordon was a straightforwardly evil maths teacher who had also taught my father in St Cyrus; to paraphrase Robert Garioch, if she's no' deid, it's time she was. She would often start the day by opening the desk drawer where she kept the registration book to find a human turd left there from the night before. New kids might be subjected not only to the traditional initiations of debagging and head-flushing, but have their satchels torched with lighter fluid, be gassed to death in locked cupboards in the science block, or be found unconscious and dangling by the lengthening loops of their underpants from the second-floor balcony, like a dead parachutist in a tree.

This was as nothing, however, compared with what was meted out to Alexander Watt. Promptly christened '40' – which turned out to be a pretty charitable assessment of his luminosity – Alexander was probably immune to pain by the time he reached us, and so his inquisitors also gleefully realized. He had watched his father burn his mother alive by tying her to a chair, soaking her in paraffin and throwing a lit cigarette at her, and he himself had nearly died when his head had been caught in a mechanical potato harrow while he was scrounging behind it for something to eat. He was still sporting a white turban bandage when he turned up at Baldragon, and he was immediately subjected to a programme of highly inventive daily torture, which by then he accepted as his fair due. He had a sidekick, Oliver Devany, a tiny dark wee boy who smelled of stale pish. In midwinter Oliver came to school only on alternate days; he had an elder brother with whom he shared a coat. I remember these two doomed souls pinned against the PE block, a white halo thickening on the wall behind them as they faced an inexhaustible fusillade of snowballs, most seeded with sharp pink gravel, and some of them just rocks rolled in snow. They stood close together, bolt upright with their hands straight by their sides, as if before a firing squad. They made no attempt to protect their faces. Conveniently, I can't remember if I took part or not.

Me and my best pal Graham had been growing heartily sick of the sight of each other throughout P7, but since we had no other friends whatsoever, we found ourselves stuck with each other. We needed to seek out our fellow nonentities with some urgency, and reflexively joined the Scripture Union the day after we started secondary school. This was doubly understandable, as we also feared for our lives. While the hopeless cases drew some of the flak, the flak factory of the estate meant there was still plenty left for the likes of us. So Graham and I sought protection, uselessly, in God and the Scripture. Being both from 'kirky' families – my grandfather was a minister in the United Free and Graham's dad a church organist – it was a fatally natural move. I had been able to recite the books of the Old Testament in fifteen seconds flat since I was seven, as a sort of fucked-up party piece, and at the time this had convinced some easily impressed old wifies that I, too, was destined for the manse. Maybe it was time to revisit that idea. Anyway things got off to an unimpressive start. My JESUS SAVES badge conspicuously did not shield me from a bucket of dirty water emptied over my head by the egregious Dougal McLeod; when I loftily forgave him and quoted Matthew 5:38, he made me eat a pan drop, earlier farted and spat on by his orc-posse. I needed a bigger badge. I reasoned that I was not praying hard enough and resolved to put in more hours.

The Scripture Union was run by a very plain young woman called Mrs Jack, with no shoulders or breasts and untamably rough fawn hair that grew in four different directions. She had a kind heart, and a husband who made the odd appearance. He was a rep for a soft drinks company, a good-looking dark-skinned guy; we reasoned somehow that she had been *rewarded* with him. Mrs Jack was soon pregnant, and he was soon dead of cancer, and her forbearance and lack of anger were both admirable and incomprehensible things to behold. This event shook me, and I was close – damn, I was close – to seeing through the whole scam, when Mrs Wilkie stood in for the grieving Mrs Jack. Small, dark-eyed, pale, with a mess of black snakes on her head, Mrs Wilkie was the last woman in the school to wear a black cloak, under which she wore white stockings and – this fact verified by a number of semi-horizontal oops-dropped-ma-pencil sources – matching suspenders. She suggested that we might like to go to an inter-school SU meeting in town with her once a week. Had she proposed we go down to the Cyrenians and tend the pustules of dying winos, I would have responded with no less alacrity.

At the SU meeting I discovered the prayer group. Now, people: at least the Buddhists are involved in some kind of genuine self-work; the dervishes are getting a little exercise; and his five-times-daily obeisances mean you rarely meet a Muslim male under the age of eighty with a bad back. By contrast, the Christian prayer group is just about the most useless gathering on this earth. It is twenty people in a room, talking for three hours to someone who isn't. The great evil of transcendental meditation was then receiving a lot of publicity, and Christian magazines were full of pictures of yogic flying, where you bounce down a line of cushions in the lotus position. In *Praise Him! Monthly*, these would be captioned as 'satanic levitation'. We were reminded frequently that prayer meetings were *not* meditation – because the self was sinful, and not to be dwelt on or enquired of. So all thinking was absolutely forbidden. (Meditation involves its cessation, of course, but few Christians ever bother to research further than the confirmation of a prejudice.) We had to concentrate on Christ the beloved and block all thought with his radiance.

And it was not enough that we had saved our own souls. We had to go forth, bear witness and recruit in the name of the Lord. We were given our urgency through the fact of our living in the Last Days. The Last Days, which seem to have started about a week after Jesus carked it, afford all born-agains their true sexual thrill. This is where they find their real freedom, their ultimate justification in behaving as if excepted from the normal human protocols, and it's what compels them to make idiots of themselves on street corners. Graham and I agreed with current thinking – given the signs, we were talking this October, at the latest. By June, the Beast would have us all tattooed with our personal barcodes, and by August we'd be listening to the frogs bouncing off our umbrellas. Fuelled up on imminent Rapture, I took to the air and shot my target converts down like the Red Baron, mentally slapping a thousand crosses on my spiritual cockpit. I had an eye for vulnerable saddos, Wullie-no-mates and nervous types, and a good line in hellfire. The fact that they lapsed or renounced after a week was no business of mine; aftercare was the Church's job. My technique was to identify their worst fear, fix them with my myopic unblinking stare, and detail how very, very much worse things were likely to get for them after the imminent Return, i.e. before Christmas. Ronny Leitch: not only will your mum never come back from Tenerife where she has buggered off with the postman, but you will be separated from the rest of your family for *all eternity*. Alasdair Bottoms: you will be the fattest boy in Hell. Gary Meldrum: if you think your spots are bad now, I can promise you that the oozing buboes that await you will cause you to look back upon this time as one of dermatological perfection. For I have read somewhere that it will be so.

It should go without saying that girls could not be recruited in this way; they either came to God for their own reasons or not at all. Nonetheless, when I was in my twenties, one of my very idlest and most reprehensible daydreams used to be starting a cult with a bunch of gullible women, plus a team of epicene/loser drone males to do the boring stuff. Alas, even my normal sexual fantasies have always had the habit of getting railroaded by walk-ons from my nightmares – especially that limping dwarf with the cattle prod – or stymied by some tiny but insurmountable practical consideration. A condom (?) will not unfurl, or a door will not lock, or a pillow refuse to lie flat, a hair will keep getting in my mouth or my partner get cramp in her foot. The religious cult fantasy, inevitably, suffered its final ithyphallic collapse at Waco. After three minutes of playing a Hef/L. Ron composite, I'd hear the FBI roll up outside with the twenty-megawatt PA, through which they started to play recordings of baby rabbits being killed – the noise they make is just like children screaming – at excruciating volume. (The other thing they played, incidentally, was Nancy Sinatra's 'These Boots Are Made for Walkin''. Does someone fill out a form for this stuff?) Inside the twenty-four children the FBI are about to murder cower screaming in corners, like baby rabbits. It's around this point that one noticed one had given up on oneself, as it were, some time ago.

Despite all this frenzy of witnessing, Graham and I were terribly aware that we were Christian Lite. I had yet to be formally converted, for one thing, and a few of my brothers were voicing concern at the speed I was taking the corners on my provisional licence. Besides, you had to take the oath before you could be Baptized in the Spirit, and Baptized in the Spirit before you could really start to climb the ranks. I envisioned my smooth progression through a sort of kyu/dan system, until I could turn my cheek with such devastating humility it would strike Dougal McLeod dead on the spot. The conversion ceremony was conducted by the nice wee minister of the Baptist church on the estate, in his underheated front room, over a cup of tea the colour of bathwater and a wee plate of Peek Freans biscuits. I merely had to repeat a standard form of words, like marriage vows. However, I misheard and said 'loving God', not 'living God', or the other way round; although he reassured me afterwards, I was long convinced my mistake had invalidated the whole thing. I mean what use is a God who doesn't attend to the letter as carefully as to the spirit?

We would hear rumours of the hard core, though, who gathered down at the Tent Mission, and some thrillingly occult goings-on no one seemed keen to discuss. They had prayer meetings that were *six hours long*. Women prophesied and frothed and bled from the nose and fainted. Men spoke in strange tongues and performed miracles and healed stuff – nosebleeds for starters, I imagined – and Graham had heard they got naked sometimes. While we were fascinated, we were happy enough, for now, to puddle around in the harmless shallows of our playground recruitment sorties, daily texts, mind-destroying visits to old folk's homes (dreaded by both parties) and daft campfire songs with 'actions'. There was always a heavy demand for new songs, and a buzz would go round whenever someone had shoehorned an obscure bit of Leviticus or Haggai into half a tune, and illustrated it with a bit of 'YMCA'-style dumb-signing that we could all learn. This was our top ten, our pop chart. 'Hey – have you heard "If with His Skirt He Do Touch Bread or Pottage"?' I found all the idiot mumming a bit hard to swallow, though, and thought continually of Play Away and Rainbow, until I realized that was the point. It was a further abasement performed before the Lord, a challenge to you to survive the furnace of your own red-faced infantilization; indeed, to emerge from it smiling and unscathed. Years later, I was walking with my own seven-year-old twins in St Andrews, and came across a group of born-agains giving it the old I'm-a-Little-Teapot semaphore outside a church. *These hands* (show hands) *that hold* (clasp imaginary tennis ball) *this heart* (point to heart) *of mine* (point to face) *have formed* (hold imaginary mug of soup) *the world* (attempt to hold planet) *since the start* (point at...the start) *of time* (point at wrist, impersonate clockwork, etc.). The boys were mystified. 'But where are all the *kids*?' asked Jamie.

Yet we were wholly content. Well, we would have been wholly content, if it hadn't been for Kevin Sergeant. Kevin was seventeen, a charismatic firebrand and brutal monobrow bully of a boy with thickly simian features and piercing BO. His armpits *sang*. (Once he told us he was late for a meeting because he had fallen asleep in the bath. I remember exchanging glances with Graham. The *bath*?) He wore pinstripe flares, skin tight at his huge thighs, and had a large range of astonishing tank tops. He tried to talk a version of RP, or more accurately to graft some kind of imaginary acrolect on top of his schemie Dundee accent. He was a man possessed of a truly terrible fanaticism. Whenever I ask myself how anyone could saw another man's head off, slowly, cack-handedly, in the name of God, I remember Kevin. I still don't know how, but I have known who.

A few said that Kevin would have been a thug had it not been for God, but they were way off the mark. Kevin was a thug anyway. He would play-fight with us sometimes in the graveyard after church, and enjoyed kneeling on our shoulders until we couldn't breathe. He would torment us with a bizarre Dundee-specific homoerotic pastime called 'three pubs and a whistle', where the challenger grabs your nipple through your shirt, wrenches it through 270 degrees, then requires that you name three local boozers and whistle a tune before they'll let go. Since neither of us could name *one* local boozer (and Graham couldn't whistle), these were especially long evenings. 'Fool' he once called me at a prayer meeting, when I expressed an opinion that conflicted slightly with his. Foolishly, I replied with Matthew 5:22 – *but whosoever shall say, Thou fool, shall be in danger of hell fire.* He took my thin neck in an excruciating Vulcan grip. *'Don't. Ever. Quote. Me.'* I looked around, waiting for the adult company to correct him, and couldn't get an eye to meet mine. The trouble is that cowardice is endemic in these communities; of *course* it is. They are terrified of their God, and if you can be cowed by that big daft nothing, you can be cowed by absolutely everything. Cowardice is their social glue. Kevin, like many of their leaders, was not terrified of his God, with whom he conversed as an equal. It followed that he could not, therefore, be cowed by anyone. He had found himself in a bully's paradise.

Despite all this, or probably because of all this, Graham and I had a serious crush on the guy, and we vied for his attention like two giggling floozies. He baited the hook and promised he would get us into the Tent Mission prayer group when he deemed us ready; that way lay Baptism in the Spirit and the keys to infinite power. I was standing at the Baldovan bus terminus one night, and praying that Kevin would materialize in time to get the bus with me to the church; he emerged from the gap in the fence just as the bus was about to pull out, and I immediately took it as a sign from God and almost fell to my knees. I mean it wasn't even a *coincidence*. Once or twice he graced me with a home visit, and I could hardly believe my luck – having Kevin himself in my own front room, with his flame-red Living Bible. (Graham and I favoured the Good News translation, with its fawn covers and cartoons. Kevin dismissed it as childish and blasphemously inaccurate.) My mother was unimpressed with him, not doubting the young man's sincerity – it was impossible, given his total-cornea unblinking monomania – but worried by his personal hygiene. I was furious with her for not loving him as we did, and the seeds were sown of a distrust of my mother and father that would eventually emerge as full-blown clinical paranoia three years later. All I smelled off Kevin was the intoxicant of his vastly deeper faith. I bought myself a flame-red Living Bible with my Christmas tokens, denounced the Good News as the work of the devil, and stopped washing.

Our praying got more competitive. I recall one recent convert, a wee old guy on the twelfth floor of the Ardler multis whom we would bombard with almost daily home visits. He must have felt like those poor refugee kids, inoculated into tea bags by thirty-three competing private charities as soon as they make it over the border. After we had eaten all his Jammie Dodgers we'd leave him propped in front of *Crossroads* and retire to his spare room to pray – to pray about any old rubbish, so long as it was for longer than Kevin had prayed at the weekend, or Raymond the day before. It was a weirdly transgressive thrill, almost sexual in quality, and it came from behaving in a way that at some level we knew was completely stupid. There was the language, for starters: prayers were conducted in the form of Elizabethan whining, with lots of random syntactic inversion and no contractions. As for the content, dearie me: *Oh Lord we do beseech that you do allow in your infinite mercy that* etc. *In return we give all our praise unto thy radiant* etc.

It seemed an odd trade, to ask the earth by appealing to the Creator's vanity. To His eternal credit, He remained as stonily immune to our flattery as He had to that of the previous sixty generations. Even then, I could see that our prayers not only had zero and possibly negative effect on global events, but that they did nothing to change even the very smallest things, stuff that surely could have been accomplished by the tug of an earlobe or a curled lip on His part. So not only did the wars rage on and Mary's tumour continue to metastasize – Kevin was not Shown the Error of his Ways, nor Malcolm stopped from Straying from the Path of Righteousness (according to Graham he had gone to the *pictures* with a *girl* who wasn't *saved* and afterwards they'd had a *drink*).

The reasons for His non-intervention were so obvious as to be not worth discussing. The trivial requests were beneath Him – it was selfish of us to have asked that He waste His time with them in the first place, and we would later apologize. We loved apologizing, especially as we had so little sin to declare these days. *O Lord forgive us that in our unworthiness and ignorance we did pridefully and foolishly* etc. The greater things were woven into a cosmic tapestry of which He had the one good view, and we were encouraged to take great pride in our ignorance of it. Christians actually spend very little time agonizing why 'a supposedly benevolent God' could allow X or Y to happen, and breezily take the tsunamis and the genocides in their stride, until their own kid gets creamed by a drunk sixteen-year-old in a stolen Fiesta. Agonizing is an agnostic pursuit. (In all this I seem to have omitted to mention faith itself. This is because faith itself was a matter of almost no consequence to any of us. Faith is something only required by casual churchgoers, not true believers, as faith is predicated on the existence of a capacity for doubt. Banish doubt and you can proceed from faith to incorruptible knowledge. Banish doubt, alas, and you also proceed directly to insanity.)

Kevin was now sufficiently impressed with our endurance worship to get us an introduction to the Tent and the Pentecostal group that met there. We were initially disappointed at the lack of theatre, nosebleeds or nudity, but their extremism made up for it. It was brilliant. Whole new arenas of previously unsuspected sin were delineated. You could sit in an empty room and think of nothing and still be sinning. I had to get to work especially hard, I realized, on sex and the room it took up in my head. I couldn't make it take up any less room, though, so I made sure that every time I thought of something it was accompanied by the shadow of its infernal punishment. This made it take up exactly twice as much room as before, and meant that the greater part of my waking hours was now given over to cursing myself, which I upgraded from pastime to vocation. It was a positive relief, then, to bound up those stairs three times a week into that yellow room to give myself a break from my self-disgust, and have some other folk be disgusted with me instead. Of course they weren't, but having gone to such lengths to convince myself that I was the embodiment of all human evil, I'd have been disappointed to find they didn't share my opinion of me. I fell in love with a fat girl with black hair and milky-blue eyes who didn't say anything, and I exhausted myself lying in the dark for hours not imagining what I didn't want to do to her.

The endless meetings were led by the kindly Jim Sprunt, a giant spider monkey of a man, with a hook nose so big he had trouble drinking properly and had to pour liquids into his face from one side. He had made his name as an exorcist, but by 1975 had pretty much cleaned up the streets, and now had the forlorn and underemployed air of a too successful pest controller. The accompaniment to our sung praises was provided by a (clearly gay, I can see now the mists have cleared) bouffanted beanpole called Brian, or Breh-hin, in Dundee camp pronunciation. He had a twelve-string guitar, the first I'd ever seen. It sounded like... it sounded like a twelve-string guitar, which is enough, if you've never heard one. Two guitars emerge from the shape of one guitar, one a heavenly high ghost of the other. They can be slightly out of tune and be even more beautiful, as the detuning makes a chorus effect. This is fortunate, as they are murder to get in tune, and usually aren't.

I was more desperate than ever to be baptized, and my undergrad status was really troubling me. After the Baptism in the Spirit, real power was conferred: you would receive one of the charismata, which were the gifts of Tongues, or the Interpretation of Tongues, Prophecy, Healing and one other one. Ventriloquism. Snakes. Who cares. Baptism in the Spirit, though, depends notoriously on God's inscrutable whim, and attempts to rush him into it tend to be counterproductive. Some members of the group had been waiting for years, and those individuals were effectively sacrificed to underline his divine capriciousness. (Again, it hasn't occurred to me until now to think how *cruel* this was, given the whole thing was completely made up.) The seemingly endless stint as Underchristian is also crucial to building up the frustration needed for the dam burst of hysterical gratitude that convinces the baptized of the reality of their experience. I think the group registered how useful such a young and zealous recruit could be, though, and I was earmarked for early promotion. I rolled up one Tuesday night when they'd booked the star preacher on the circuit – an appealing, dumpy little guy from Aberdeen (affectionately known as the Wee Pope, in a touching demonstration of their genuine lack of interest in sectarian matters). His shtick was pretty much identical to the others', just much louder and more quivery: where some would shake from their lack of conviction, he shook with an excess of it. He spoke quite normally, but when fully inflated with the Spirit sang in a high-pitched, heavily vibratoed monotone that drooped at the end of each phrase, like a ghost from *Scooby-Doo*.

We started prayer and were an hour or so into our private deranged chunterings when I heard him walking among us. The footsteps stopped behind me. 'And who-oo-oo-oo is this young ma-aa-aa-n?' I heard him ask our leader and I knew it was my night. There was then a 'laying on of hands', which is to say a few folk laid their hands on you, and lo the Paraclete descended among us, and I was filled with the Holy Spirit like what were – as Kevin would say – the Apostles at Pentecost, and I did speak with the tongues of the heavenly orders. I stood with my arms frozen in that classic attitude of big reception, like Bellini's *St Francis in Ecstasy*. Grace descended. I wept, I shook, and my cup did runneth over. I'm sitting here blushing at the memory.

When the queues for the charismata form, everyone except the genuinely mad (Invisible Dave, whom God had given a special hat) or the power mad (Kevin) line up for Tongues. The Gift of Tongues is technically identical to the fire that descended at Pentecost, which allowed the Apostles to wind the clock back pre-Babel and talk to all men in their own language. You might speak, it was said, in Polish or Malay or Catalan, or maybe even the big one, Middle Aramaic. Everyone of course aspired to Middle bloody Aramaic, though even then it was a point of common scholarship that Jesus would have spoken as much or more Greek. Since no one had a clue how it sounded, it was frequently claimed. I did once hear someone attempt Spanish, hilariously, and it really was all *dónde está la estación por favor*, with a bit of ying-tong-tiddle-I-po what-the-hell thrown in. No one ever wanted to speak Sanskrit or Navajo, i.e. anything heathen or primitive. Mercifully there was a get-out, a dignified option, and almost all of us flung ourselves at it. You might also speak in the Tongues of the Angels.

Angeloglossia were, on the strength of our performance, a whole bunch of mutually incomprehensible dialects with a lot of labials. They clearly had a Babel of their own up there. The clouds must continually resound with the Angelic for *you what?* and, among the wags, *that's easy for you to say*. Some, however, were very beautiful and sounded just like real languages, and indeed may have been, if not of this planet; they had a consistent music and phraseology that in their repetitions and inflections must have converged here and there on something real, somewhere in the cosmos (unlike the monkey at the typewriter that will *never* write a line of Shakespeare, even given an hour for every subatomic particle in the universe). I knew that I had just heard in *santanderi tro mestfira li menor li menoschka tre perrissa* a snatch of a laundry list or match report or love poem from some long-forgotten enclave in Transylvania, or somewhere deep in the Beehive cluster. Others were plain echolalic gibberish, and sounded like the ombly-jombly-wombly bits in Edward Lear, and it was hard to keep a straight face.

Whatever it might have sounded like, my own was a fairly satisfying affair, as my tongue was liberated – weirdly, beyond any freedom I could permit it in private – to make all the nice syllables I had ever dreamed of. It was, in the midst of the most psychologically damaging experience of my life, wildly cathartic; I still think there is a sound secular therapy in there somewhere. Kevin's tongues, on the other hand, were another matter. Kevin spoke in the dialect of some retarded infernal troll. It mostly consisted of two words: *Oombara coombara oombara coombara oombara coombara...* I was both terrified and embarrassed for him. I was amazed no one had ever pulled him aside to tell him he was clearly talking bollocks, and could he either shut up or make more of an effort.

There was one thing I looked forward to, though. After the interminable bearing witness; after the prophesy of such arse-covering vagueness it made Nostradamus sound like a PowerPoint presentation; after the endless prayers cobbled together from the same handful of stock phrases; after the comically hopeless attempts to heal the sick (I remember a pair of crutches falling away from one poor bugger, in slow motion, like the support cranes on an Apollo rocket; for one glorious half-second it seemed that he would stand unaided – before he hit the floor in a puddle of limbs, as if his puppeteer had suddenly remembered a lunch appointment); after the gabble, jabber and gibber of tongues... after all that, someone would start to sing. It would begin with one person, always a woman, singing one long note, to which everyone gradually ascended like a slow, lovely air-raid siren; then we began to harmonize, every man or woman still singing in their own strange tongue, but the vowels lengthening until they were singing together, one supple and rippling vowel, moving through its formants like the spectrum through the skin of a salmon. It was a symbol beyond anything we were equipped to understand, but we were wonderfully in its grip. It sounded identical, I discovered later, to Free Church psalm singing in the Western Isles, where the precentor sings a line of Gaelic to have it echoed and harmonized and embroidered by the congregation, their shifting layers like one cold Atlantic wave slowly breaking on another.

Long after I extracted myself from the Church – a chortle-free tale that can wait, trust me – I heard that Kevin had been thrown out for heresy, having unwisely claimed for himself the gift of healing, and suggesting to several incurable paraplegics that it was only their weak faith that was standing between them and a trial for Lochee Violet. Whether this was true or not, I warmed to him all over again. For one thing I was delighted that you still *got* heretics, just as I was delighted to find, in a wee sweetshop in Thurso last year, that you still got Cowan's Egg and Milk Chews. I gather they let him back in after a month or so, though. Honestly; nothing's what it was. I mean how on earth could Giordano Bruno or Jan Hus have been expected to make their reputations from ten minutes in the sin bin?

Inevitably, though, Kevin has disappointed me. A cursory Google reveals a man – and what reason do I have to disbelieve this – now selflessly devoted to his faith, and to community projects in some of the poorest parts of Asia. I dare say he was facing down his adolescent demons in his own way. Pathetically, I have only just realized as I write this that *he was a boy himself.* Whoever he is now, I hope he has lost his bomb-proof self-certainty and cross-hair singularity of purpose. A shark's most characteristic psychological attributes shouldn't be ours. But I could still weep for the rest of them, for those teenagers on the TV on Sunday mornings, one hand on their heart, one hand raised, their eyes closed, their fixed smile, that slow, perverse *shaking* of the head in what they think is deep affirmation but is no more than a disavowal of the world and of themselves, of their own brain's plea to simply be permitted to *think*, and use the faculty it spent three and a half billion years evolving. ∎

THE SILKWORMS

Janet Frame

ILLUSTRATION BY GEORGE BUTLER

If only, he thought, I were God looking from my door upon completeness.

Before I die.

He was not old, only fifty-five. His hair was thin and faded, like desert grass, flattened by secret pressures from the sky. His head was land; within it he felled forests of beech, rimu, kauri, burned the scrub, hacked manuka for fences, measured and set the boundaries for paddocks.

'Poor Edgar,' the neighbours said. 'The past has sprinkled salt on his tail, has trapped him in important flight.'

Only it was not that way at all. He was not a bird. Was he a cat, then? Had he swallowed the past, licking it from his life as a cat licks its fur until it winds into a ball inside, compact, soft, a nest ball that causes pain?

Oh whatever was the matter with Edgar? Cat, bird, human being: it was yesterday that was the matter, and it was no use saying to him, Don't groom your memory day after day on the hearth until you swallow it and it hurts you, stops your life!

Every morning he sunbathed, lying naked on a rug beside the east wall of the house, only a few feet away from the tomatoes (the stout Russian variety), the clump of garlic, the potatoes numerously leaved like Bibles, with the small bloodless fruit beneath; the swollen-veined cabbages; airy parsley.

He sunbathed for an hour, taking stock of the sun and the secret growth of his vegetables.

Then he would go inside, dress, and using a pencil upon green paper because green was said to be kind to the eyes, he would sit at his home-made table to write his work of literature. He leaned over the table, his shoulders hunched, his face tensed, as if he were in a lavatory. The words came dropping from him tight, and round, and hard.

The compressed words came dropping slowly from him like childhood bullets. All morning he worked, writing, crossing out, writing again, and afterwards typing the fragment he had made, adding it to the pile of green sheets, counting them carefully, reckoning how many more he must squeeze from his head before he completed the work of literature.

Sometimes when he was reluctant to begin working he would sit on the stool near his kitchen window and look out, at the postman passing, throwing the letters in the old biscuit tin which Edgar had put inside the hedge as a letter box; at the paper boy cycling by, aiming the paper through the gap in the hedge that served as a gate, on to the narrow path. Or he would watch people hurrying to work, to catch the bus and the ferry to the city. He would see his next-door neighbour whose face, on Mondays, had a satisfied expression – had he not mowed the lawn in the weekend with the new electric mower, cut down a troublesome tree in his garden with his new electric saw, built a kitchen table for his wife from the Do-It-Yourself kit, and then had time to spend the whole of Sunday afternoon with his wife and three children at one of the East Coast Bays? His father, who lived in a little self-contained hut on the property, had not accompanied them: he was growing old; he was better at home in the sun with a handkerchief over his face.

Edgar looked from his window and saw the past. He had known the area when he was a child. He could not accept the cutting back of the bush nor the rows of white-toothed villas biting into the beach where once he had played under the pohutukawa trees, and where, in the depression days, he had roamed the sand in search of food – cabbages, onions, cast overboard from the trading vessels.

So he lived alone in his house. He grew his hedge high. He pursued his work of literature.

It must be that I am growing old, he said to himself.

It was breakfast time. He had sunbathed, and was drinking a cup of tea while he read the *Critique of Pure Reason*, propping the book against a half-filled jar of preserved peaches.

It's strange about the forest in my head, he thought. I remember it. Down in the King Country on holiday. I went into the farm kitchen and they said to me, What is that terrible look on your face? They demanded to know, as if my seeing the bush fire had collected a fortune which showed in my face and which caused them fear and envy that it was not their prize also.

Come on, what is that terrible look on your face?

Own up, they were saying, own up, where is the gold mine?

I cried. I never knew what the look was. Have I a look on my face now? If so it is not fear at seeing my flesh perish, my leaves slowly writhe in the grip of fire and progress?

He who desires completeness is against progress. There is no completeness while Time continues to provide a future.

I have an engineering look on my face now, a scientific look. In the south after the earthquake they rebuilt the city and reclaimed the land which the shock cast up from the sea. I am reclaiming a certain completeness before I die. Does the sun twist the necks of sunflowers, like a screw-top vision to preserve the molten fruit?

When I was a boy I kept silkworms, from their birth to their death.

Therefore one day Edgar put on his best pants, tied with string at the waist, his grey pullover, his Roman sandals, and his old stained gabardine, and travelling in the bay bus down to the harbour, he bought his ticket for the ferry, and sitting outside in the sun he crossed the harbour to the abominable city where he bought twelve silkworms in a small cardboard box from the pet store in the street next to the main street.

In the main street were the fashionable stores; then came, like the other side of the moon, the coin, the dream, the places which sold second-hand clothing – men's crumpled collapsed suits, women's shapeless floral dresses to which time and the salt-filled light of the harbour sun had given a mimic sheen of newness, a wild brightness; as if a lifetime were crushed between the two streets, like wheat between stones. The pet shop was next to a second-hand dealer's and a vacant shop with the door boarded up and the windows broken in a star shape revealing that core of darkness which centres itself in holes, gaps of light, the beginning of tunnels, and open doorways at night.

The silkworms had been thriving in the window of the pet shop, next to odorous guinea pigs and white mice with rosebud skin. Edgar bought twelve silkworms in a small cardboard box and returning immediately to the ferry wharf he boarded the next ferry across the harbour and was soon home, collecting on the way a bigger cardboard chocolate box from the dairy at the corner of his street.

It must be done, Edgar thought, exactly as it was when I was a child.

I am in my middle fifties, he said.

I am alone, he said.

I have loved and lost and won. I am not a Biblical character; I have no issue.

Most of his friends were married and had borne children who in their turn had borne children, in historic continuity. He felt himself omitted from history, as if in taking up with the marching generations in the beginning of his life he had journeyed so far and then been trapped in a pothole, up to his neck. His head mattered, the bush fires in his head, his work of literature, his reading, and now the silkworms through which he could control history itself; birth, copulation, death.

He put the silkworms in their chocolate box and went thoughtfully out to the garden. He stroked the plump tomatoes, already striped with yellow. He lifted the leaves of the wandering Chinese gooseberry and considered the hairy ball shape. The real sign of age, he thought, is when you lean over and your balls hang down as far as the earth.

He crossed then to the two pawpaw trees. He had never grown pawpaws until now. He hoped that soon they would produce fruit. Meanwhile, they needed help. One was male, the other female; there was no communication between them apart from the haphazard dancing of bees who did not understand at all. Very carefully Edgar removed pollen from the stamen of the male tree and performed his daily task of fertilizing the female pawpaw.

When it bears fruit, he said, I will eat the fruit for breakfast while I read *The Faerie Queene* or the *Critique of Pure Reason* or Gibbon's *Decline and Fall*.

Before I die, he said, I will get once more through Gibbon.

The pawpaw contracted a terrible disease. Its leaves withered from the edges towards the heart of the leaf; its young trunk was encrusted with silver scales; it was playing host to a species of death.

Edgar went up to the house and sat alone all day at his desk; he was so bewildered that he could write nothing.

But there were still the silkworms. They were flourishing now. Edgar had canvassed the neighbours for mulberry leaves.

'Excuse me, I notice you have a mulberry tree in your garden. I wonder would you be so kind as to supply me with leaves?'

'Have your children started keeping silkworms too?'

'Yes, for silkworms.'

'It's not as if they supply much silk.'

'Would you then be so kind? I'll try not to disturb you when I call.'

The woman had looked hard at Edgar, trying to sum him up. He seemed a disreputable character, and one didn't want such people coming back and forth in one's garden with the excuse of gathering mulberry leaves for silkworms. On the other hand some folk who look disreputable often turn out to be quite distinguished, well known, with talks over the radio and invitations to cocktail parties in the University set. Oh, how was one to know?

The woman looked still harder at Edgar. She decided that he was disreputable. Yet with a feeling of being generous she said, 'Of course you can have the mulberry leaves.'

She thought, The silkworms don't live all that long.

She sighed. Why isn't it planned for us?

So Edgar found his supply of leaves for the silkworms.

The female pawpaw tree died. Edgar dug it out, removed the tiny shrivelled fruit to show to friends ('my pawpaws, my first ever') and burned the tree in the rubbish fire at the bottom of the garden.

The orange tree and the lemon tree bore their glowing lamps to the funeral. When night came the smoke still hung in the air and the crickets and grasshoppers continued their nether song, for strings.

I am in my middle fifties, Edgar said. I have no issue.

He put out the flames, for the world at night must be made safe from fire, and he went inside to bed. The silkworms were in their box on the table in the kitchen next to his bedroom. Even from where he lay he could hear them at their compulsive, continuous, desperate meal: a giant sound in the night as of crackling twigs and breaking boughs. Edgar dared to calculate the level of commotion were the silkworms the size of men. He shuddered at the noise of the falling world. He got out of bed, went to the silkworms, and lifting one of them on to the table, he squashed it with the end of a spoon: a green stain oozed from it. Disgusted, he threw the dead worm in the tin under the sink where he kept the scraps and the used tea leaves. Then with the noise of the marathon meal echoing and swelling about him he returned to his bed, buttoned the top button of the old grey shirt that he wore at night, and lay on his back, stiffly, with the skin of his face damp, slowly relaxing into the erased mask of sleep where people who witness it like to impress a fancied innocence, not realizing that for the night the years of experience have retired within, to rage their havoc among dreams.

And while Edgar slept (how transparent his eyelids seemed, like gateways to alternate sight! And see, at the corner of his mouth, the tiny stream of saliva flowing from its source in the dark cavern!) the silkworms wide awake pursued their frenzied meal.

The noise of the tireless mandibles pierced Edgar's sleep, entered like clashing swords into each dream – and Edgar had many dreams that night. He dreamed of his garden, the tomatoes, the Chinese gooseberries, the two pawpaw fruits and the diseased tree; he dreamed of his work of literature, of bush fires, gold mines; of postmen who cast a lichen over each letter in order to prevent him from opening it – it changed to an oyster growth, his fingers bled touching the sharp shells; he was under the sea, safe from fire; one side of his face was diseased; one side of his body was diseased, only his balls hung like pearls; there was a noise of machines; the sea dried, the salt stayed in heaps tall as mountains; the quick-motion trees sprang into growth, the machines commenced their meal, eating through driftwood houses and trees with their tops in the sky, swallowing shadows and the sun, but the sun stuck in their crops, they burned to death.

Lily Hogan has a dress of silk.

Some people save: I could never save. I kept silkworms.

Why do you choose green leaves to write your work of literature?

Do you not realize the danger to green leaves, with silkworms in the house?

He woke, sweating. The one hundred and seventy-two pages were in order, safe.

Edgar's friends came to visit him at night. He stood, separated from them by the table, and lectured to them; on the devouring evils of progress, on Russian tomatoes, Gibbon's *Decline and Fall*, misplaced power stations, the real distance between the head and the tail of a serpent or cycle; and silkworms.

One evening they noticed that he was winding sheets of his green writing paper into cone shapes.

'The silkworms have shed their skins the required number of times,' he said. 'I notice that one of them has begun to wave its head about and shed from its jaws a thin thread of gold silk. You see,' he said, continuing in his excited, important manner, 'it is ready to weave. I shall drop the silkworms one by one into these cones of paper, attach each one to the wall by a pin – so – and let the silkworms complete their spinning. Soon they will disappear in a cloud of golden silk; and lie in hiding; I shall unwind their silk—'

He was yesterday; it was a lesson he had learned. He was repeating it.

Edgar's friends watched him in embarrassed dismay. He was a bow-tied courier who had learned the language although he no longer lived in the country. He was conducting them, as tourists, through the territory of his past without apparently realizing that it had changed, that all things visible or invisible are only shadows attending shapes of Change under the Sun of Time; they shrivel like shadows of two pawpaws at noon.

But of course Edgar knew this: Edgar was wise. He continued his lecture, pinning the cone shapes to the wall beneath the Christmas card from Spain which said PAX, PAX.

Some days later when the silkworms had finished spinning and were settled in their cocoons with doors and windows shut, and had changed to pupae, Edgar unwound the silk from each one on to strips of cardboard, and each time as he reached the boudoir at the end of the maze he was confronted by the naked black-eyed unseemly monster who trembled and shrank from his touch. The sensitivity alarmed him. What was its purpose? A fly might brush his own cheek, rain fall upon his skin, he could walk in rooms, bumping into furniture, enduring the hazards and encounters of the living and the dead, yet not flinch or shrink. By what right was the chrysalis so privileged in sensitivity? Why did it recoil from him?

Nevertheless, in spite of his envy, very gently he wrapped the cruelly exposed pupae in cotton wool, placed them once again in the chocolate box from which he had cleaned the waste, and left them in peace (was it peace?) until they should emerge as moths. He was relieved not to have to look upon the ugly sensitive creatures while they accomplished their metamorphosis.

Then one morning when he decided to unwrap one of them from its cotton wool he found that the welted boot-polish-brown tough skin had hardened and shrivelled and a moth lay on the soft white bed, its beautifully patterned wings (circles of dark suns) limp, fresh and moist. In all, nine moths had emerged; two of the pupae had kept their original shape, tapering at both ends like coffins, one of which enclosed a dead half-moth, the other, nothing. Tenderly Edgar picked up the nine moths and put them in another box where soon the males crawled towards the females and all were paired except the odd one which stayed in a corner, feebly trying out the wings which it would never use for flight. Hours passed, and still the moths clung together; then as night came each male moth fell from its mate, and died, its wings now sheenless and crumpled. With the slight strength remaining to them the female moths crawled upon the small sheets of cardboard which Edgar provided for each one, and soon the eggs in neat rows, like tiny white running stitches, were laid upon the cardboard, and then one by one the female moths also died, with the glitter dust rubbed from their wings. Had they known that wings are for flying?

Edgar had stayed by them in their travail of lust and their death. They had no towers in their heads, he was aware of that, nor lighthouses to guide the homing thoughts, nor wrecked thoughts dismantled by the imperative tides coming and going to trade salt and tears in all four corners of breathing feeling and knowing.

The sordid spectacle depressed him at last. Why had the chrysalis been so responsive and the wings so beautifully patterned? Why had there been wings at all?

But it was the cycle, it was the completeness.

Nothing has changed, Edgar said. What new event is written into their history? None. Where is their future? Nowhere. Are they against or for progress?

It was dark when Edgar took the box outside down to the rubbish heap and sprinkled the dead moths upon the ashes of the diseased pawpaw. Then, carrying the sheets of cardboard with their tiny fertile full stops (ends of chapters, heads beneath the exclamatory swords, tiny marks standing waist high above the embryo semicolon) he went into the garden, dug a hole, and buried the eggs.

When the hot weather comes, he said to himself, I will dig them up and hatch out the new silkworms in the sun... get more mulberry leaves... another chocolate box...

He went inside the house, and unwinding each thread of silk he began to plait all the threads. Massed, their gold acquired a languor and sheen. He hung the plaited silk rope upon the wall beneath the Spanish Christmas card which said PAX, PAX.

That's all, he said. I have stood in the doorway, like God.

I kept silkworms when I was a child. Nothing has changed. The bush fire still burns and the people cry for the share of it which they see in my face, Where did you get that terrible look on your face? What have you seen?

Tell us quickly.

There is no new magic.

Where's the gold mine? What are we doing with ourselves, birth copulation and death and no use to make of our wings?

When Edgar had buried the eggs he went to his bedroom, put on his grey shirt, and got into bed. He slept deeply, without dreams that cared to acknowledge themselves to his waking curiosity. And next morning he woke, sunbathed at the east wall, read the *Critique of Pure Reason*, propping it against the sugar bowl, and then sat at his table with the leaf-green sheets of paper before him, and his HB pencil, sharpened, in his hand.

I should be satisfied now, he said, and looked at the mass of plaited silk, burnished by the sun.

Then the fire raced through the forest and chains swung from the sky. He leaned his head in his hands.

If only, he thought, I were God looking from my door upon completeness. ∎

'Richardson has a transporting voice and the journey his characters make is profound.' *Sunday Times*

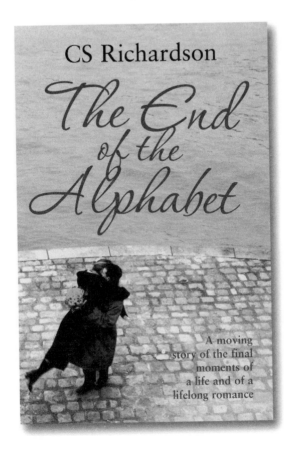

WINNER OF A COMMONWEALTH WRITERS' PRIZE

'An elegant fable, charmingly written, and a tender, grateful paean to time, love and literature.' *Guardian*

'A story of tender romance and unexpected discovery that lifts and breaks the heart.' *Saga*

Portobello

www.portobellobooks.com

Available in paperback now

'*A Country in the Moon* is literary travel writing at its best: elegiac, informative and profound. It's probably the best travel book I will read this year'
Jim Blackburn, *Wanderlust* 'Book of the Month'

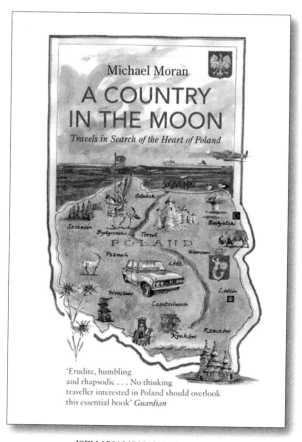

ISBN 9781847081049 · Paperback

'As much cultural history as conventional travel narrative . . . This lively and intelligent book is stuffed with original material that is both fascinating and quite new to most people in the West'
Robert Carver, *Times Literary Supplement*

'Wonderful' Giles Foden, *Condé Nast Traveller*

www.granta.com

THE ROAD

Photographs by Mimi Mollica

Words by Elena Baglioni

It is not always acknowledged that development is a disruptive, sometimes irrational, process, but these photographs make clear the chaos of Dakar's urban sprawl as it expands westwards in a mass of concrete, commerce, transport and people, all part of Senegal's complex socio-economic transition. That process includes the construction of a new highway that rips though the centre of Dakar and heads west for thirty-two kilometres, connecting the capital to towns in the Senegalese hinterland, as well as the planned airport at Diass.

Once the road is completed, it is predicted that the fortunes of Dakar's port will revive, bus journeys will speed up, commuters will get to work more easily, rice, groundnuts, oil and other basic supplies will circulate effortlessly, trade will blossom, development will boom and wealth will, in that familiar phrase, 'trickle down'. So expectations are high: the road will provide a link between two very different spaces – the capital and *the rest* – somehow softening the divide that still characterizes much of Africa.

So far, only the first seven kilometres have been finished. The remaining twenty-five, together with new roundabouts, interchanges, viaducts and bridges, should be ready in 2011. The architect of this huge construction is a state still in pursuit of a 1960s development dream.

The *autoroute* was proposed, following independence in 1960, by Senegal's first president, Léopold Senghor, who believed that 'progress' lay in a peculiar form of African socialism linked to his country's French inheritance. But by the 1970s this dream was fading. By 1980, with the widespread debt crisis in the global south, the World Bank made it clear that socialism was the wrong approach and the new president, Abdou Diouf, was forced to adopt another path. Like other African countries, the new government was obliged to pursue development policies that curtailed state intervention and were based on the free market. This was a drastic about-turn. Twenty years later, in 2000, the Senegalese went to the ballot box and voted for change. A new president, Abdoulaye Wade, was elected, but there is still much debate about whether change has arrived.

Under President Wade, the Dakar highway was identified as an urgent national priority. And, like other recent schemes, he assigned it to a special agency created to 'assist the Senegalese President in conceiving and implementing the policy regarding the promotion of investments and major projects'. This agency, set up in 2000, is directly linked to the president's office and acts as an extension of the government, attracting new investors for private-public partnerships. With regard to the *autoroute* project, the agency deals with all the financial arrangements, including those with the World Bank and Chinese and Portuguese companies involved in the project.

In Africa, in the name of better (or 'good') governance, official institutions are commonly circumvented and policy-making transferred to alternative hands. The World Bank, the International Monetary Fund and other Western institutions take an active part in everyday decision making. One spectacular example is the new agenda for global poverty reduction for Africa, rarely conceived in the national parliaments, but rather dealt with through a series of 'external' workshops and seminars. The saga of the Dakar highway might be another illustration of the influence of recent Western development practices where the African state is frequently disregarded.

Dakar is now one enormous building site. As well as the work on the new highway, three other large development sites further complicate urban circulation. Every day, citizens are confronted with unexpected diversions, improvised roundabouts, as well as inanimate and animate obstacles. The air is saturated with sand and dust and, when the Harmattan (the dry, dusty trade wind) blows from the Sahara, it becomes a thick, almost physical barrier. The constantly changing landscape fosters a sense of revolution for all those living and working in the capital, including the daily commuters. But their troubles must be set against the sparkling vision of a future Champs-Elysées.

Mountains of different-coloured fabrics, billboards and seemingly irrational concrete pedestrian walkways all contribute to the messy landscape of construction and change. On the ground pavements have still not been laid, but at least the sand makes their absence more comfortable. While Dakar is being reshaped, the Senegalese react to the new road in different ways. Basically, they adjust.

Due to the scarcity of resources, people occupy any space that is temporarily abandoned before it is handed over to the voracious excavators. Male and female joggers take advantage of the transitional landscape that offers them a rare, uninterrupted stretch of track. On one side of the road, footballers have marked off their pitch with tyres.

Every day an army of street vendors – the new *autoroute* businessmen – set out their wares on the roadside. In one particular sector on the northern border, the backdrop to the road is a green curtain patterned with bougainvillea, frangipani and small baobab trees. Shepherds sell their beloved sheep. For them the road is a good marketplace: drivers draw up and, after a round of hard but cordial bargaining, load the animals into the backs of their cars. On their way they can also buy flowers, tropical plants, trees, even bonsai. Then in the midst of people bargaining, building, chatting, cooking, doing the laundry, resting, playing, running, walking, or merely hanging around, some also find a sandy corner to unroll their small carpet and engage in a five-minute dialogue with God.

Mimi Mollica's photographs lead us to a fundamental question: are the citizens being swept away by this transition, or are they really making this new space their own? As the daily invasion of vehicles and human beings increases, little is known about the displaced, past or future (official government estimates point to more than 4,000 families). Not long ago, there were houses, trees, boutiques, garages and other commercial buildings standing here. Soon, the activities of those currently trading on the roadside will also be interrupted, when the road becomes a toll highway, enclosed by walls to keep out everything but commuter traffic. Many will benefit from faster, more efficient circulation, but some will not. Although no decision has yet been made about the tolls, it is certain that the cost of travelling and commuting will increase. Certainly one section of the population will be unable to afford the cost of development. For these road users, the rural–urban divide will remain pretty much as it is. ∎

National Theatre

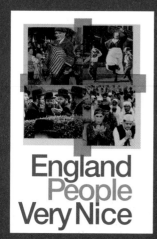

England
People
Very Nice

England People Very Nice

a new play by Richard Bean

A riotous journey through four waves of immigration, entering the chaotic world of Bethnal Green.

This new comedy by Richard Bean follows a pair of star-crossed lovers from the 17th century to today.

From 4 February

Travelex
£10 Tickets

TRAVELEX £10 TICKETS
Sponsored by

Travelex worldwide money

Media Partner

THE TIMES

Television Media Partner

skyARTS

Burnt by the Sun

photo © Corbis

Burnt by the Sun

by Peter Flannery, from the screenplay by Nikita Mikhalkov and Rustam Ibragimbekov

A story of sexual jealousy, political backstabbing and revenge, set at the dawn of Stalin's Great Terror.

Peter Flannery's previous work includes *Our Friends in the North* and *The Devil's Whore*.

From 24 February

020 7452 3000 • no booking fee • Select your seat online

nationaltheatre.org.uk

ARTS COUNCIL ENGLAND

GRANTA
THE MAGAZINE OF NEW WRITING

If you enjoy good writing, you'll love Granta – fiction, reportage, memoir, biography and photography five times a year

Subscribe to *Granta* or buy an annual subscription for a friend and receive, with our compliments, a *Granta* special-edition **MOLESKINE®** notebook

Subscribe online at **www.granta.com** or by **Freephone 0500 004 033** or fill in the **back of this card** and send to us

'With each new issue, Granta *enhances its reputation for presenting, in unequalled range and depth, the best contemporary writers in journalism and fiction.*'
SUNDAY TIMES

Yes, I would like to take out an annual subscription to *Granta* and receive a complimentary *Granta* special-edition **MOLESKINE®** notebook

YOUR ADDRESS FOR DELIVERY

Your address:

TITLE: INITIAL: SURNAME:

ADDRESS:

POSTCODE:

TELEPHONE:

EMAIL:

Billing address if different:

TITLE: INITIAL: SURNAME:

ADDRESS:

POSTCODE:

TELEPHONE: EMAIL:

NUMBER OF SUBSCRIPTIONS	DELIVERY REGION	PRICE	DIRECT DEBIT PRICE (UK ONLY)
☐	UK	£34.95	£29.95
☐	Europe	£39.95	
☐	Rest of World	£45.95	All prices include delivery

I would like my subscription to start from:
☐ the current issue   ☐ the next issue

YOUR TWELVE-MONTH SUBSCRIPTION WILL INCLUDE FIVE ISSUES

PAYMENT DETAILS

☐ I enclose a cheque payable to '*Granta*' for £ _____ for _____ subscriptions to *Granta*

☐ Please debit my ☐ MASTERCARD ☐ VISA ☐ AMEX for £ _____ for _____ subscriptions

NUMBER ☐☐☐☐ ☐☐☐☐ ☐☐☐☐ ☐☐☐☐   SECURITY CODE ☐☐☐

EXPIRY DATE ☐☐ / ☐☐   SIGNED   DATE

Instructions to your bank or building society to pay Direct Debit

DIRECT Debit

TO THE MANAGER:

(BANK OR BUILDING SOCIETY NAME)

ADDRESS:

POSTCODE:

ACCOUNT IN NAME(S) OF:

SIGNED: DATE:

BANK/BUILDING SOCIETY ACCOUNT NUMBER
☐☐☐☐☐☐☐☐

SORT CODE
☐☐ ☐☐ ☐☐

Instructions to your bank or building society Please pay Granta Publications Direct Debits from the account detailed on this instruction subject to the safeguards assured by the Direct Debit Guarantee. I understand that this instruction may remain with Granta and, if so, details will be passed electronically to my bank/ building society.

Banks and building societies may not accept Direct Debit instructions from some types of account

ORIGINATORS IDENTIFICATION
| 9 | 1 | 3 | 1 | 3 | 3 |

☐ Please tick this box if you would like to receive special offers from *Granta*
☐ Please tick this box if you would like to receive offers from organizations selected by *Granta*

Please return this form to: **Granta Subscriptions, PO Box 2068, Bushey, Herts, WD23 3ZF, UK, call Freephone 0500 004 033** or go to **www.granta.com**

Please quote the following promotion code when ordering online: **GBIUK105**

OF EARTHLY LOVE

Altán Walker

*Altán Walker spent many years working on a highly ambitious
and original debut novel,* Of Earthly Love. *In December 2007,
overwhelmed by depression, she took her own life. Here, her
literary agent, Georgia Garrett, introduces two extracts from
the novel and describes her arresting talent.*

About ten years ago, Altán Walker wrote to me on the advice of a
mutual friend from university. We had both been undergraduates
at Cambridge in the mid-Eighties and I remembered her vaguely: a tall
Northern Irish girl, very animated, blonde. She had written the
beginning of her first novel, she said. It was to be called *Of Earthly Love*
– would I like to take a look at it? I had switched from being an editor
to a literary agent and was keen to discover new writers, an eagerness
that often disappeared once I started reading their work. There have
been only a very few occasions when an unpublished writer's
manuscript has made my scalp prickle and my heart race, but this was
one of them.

I read the chapters Altán had sent in one sitting. The narrative voice
commanded attention from the opening lines: it was arch and
diamond-hard, and yet warmth curled through it, like laughter barely
suppressed. The chapters themselves were not all consecutive; there
was one that was evidently from later on in the novel, a sexual
encounter that seethed with dark nihilistic anger and disgust, but still

with that ripple of comedy. I thought the material was brilliant, and that I'd never read anything like it.

Of Earthly Love was to be, according to Altán, 'a story of adultery, a love story about a girl and two men'. It was set in the 1980s and the girl was Blair, a twenty-three-year-old Northern Irish law-graduate who has come to Dublin to study Irish law with a view to qualifying as a solicitor. She shares a flat with Aoife, a young woman who is also a solicitor, and has fallen in love with Richard, an elegant and imperturbable barrister, rather older than her. But there is a problem which Altán's outline for the novel describes thus:

> Richard adheres devoutly and almost nobly to a typical masculine credo whereby freedom is God, all domestic virtues are vulgar and the preservation of personal liberty is man's first duty in life... Richard is certainly fond of Blair but is not building his life around her and has no intention of getting married any time soon. Worse still, he really doesn't believe in fidelity and goes to bed with a tacky little actress while Blair is away for the weekend.

In the novel, Blair storms off in search of revenge, encounters a married man, Patrick, and becomes embroiled in a devastating affair with him which threatens his marriage and her sanity as she begins 'to combust internally through the heat of obsessive love'.

The material was written in a highly stylized, incantatory, poetic prose and it shifted register effortlessly; from high seriousness to delirious larky comedy to brutal, lacerating, psychological truth. The intellect that underpinned it fascinated me. Altán's frame of literary reference took in Celtic myth, Irish epic poetry, Roman law, the Bible, paganism, nineteenth-century novels, American movies and *Hello!* magazine, and she expanded on it in frequent letters than ran to three, five, ten pages – and once, memorably, a fifty-five page 'treatment' of the novel, sent for my safekeeping in case it was ever made into a film. Even more impressive than the meta-commentary on her writing was that Altán always knew just how much of it to put into the novel itself: in one of her first letters to me, she elaborated on her underlying themes: 'Richard and Blair think they are in *Les Liaisons Dangereuses*, style-bible of Enlightenment love; and Blair later thinks she is in *Anna Karenina*, style-bible of tragic Romantic love', but you didn't need to know that to be transfixed by the unfolding story.

In 2001, I sold Altán's novel to a publisher, Philip Gwyn Jones of HarperCollins, on the basis of the early chapters, and we embarked upon a happy and fruitful three-way editorial process. A representative postcard of Philip's from the period reads:

> I've just had this latest instalment from Altán and I pass on a copy here. It comes with a terrifically buoyant letter from her in which, among other glories, she declares herself 'an ancient in sensibility', me likewise, but you, Georgia, are a *modern*. I shall now take the afternoon to work out what this means.

But still Altán found it hard to sustain her confidence in the material. She would post me an alternative first chapter and then follow up the next day with a call. Had I received a package from her? Yes, it was here on my desk, not yet opened. She would then instruct me not to read it before sending a further revision. I would duly read both versions and sometimes the discredited one would seem to me much the better and I would dare to say so. 'Didn't I tell you to destroy that one?' She never remained irritated for long and we would soon find ourselves discussing the chapter's merits and demerits – a conversation that usually resulted in a brand-new version winging its way to me some days later.

It was frustrating, but also exhilarating, to be that close to a great writer's creative process, but for Altán, as her mood slid downward in autumn 2003, it was becoming unbearable:

> It will not surprise you to learn that I have probably written this book ten times over in terms of the number of words I generate but these are disconnected bursts of different modes and moods which don't 'cut together' into a uniform whole. Still worse, I have often sat, like a pianist endlessly playing scales and ephemeral beautiful improvisations, writing and rewriting the same passage over and

over again in a different way, with different images, producing some
remarkable literary artefacts: *all of which I throw away.*

Altán suffered from a devastating mood disorder and all the years
I knew her she see-sawed from periods of unspeakable darkness
to times when she was the most light-filled, life-affirming person I
have ever met. When she was in the grip of depression she was
uncontactable. She wasn't on email; she gave me no phone number,
no address. For months all I would receive would be a fax – dateless,
addressless – with a couple of matter-of-fact lines about her despair.
Then she would resurface, usually in the spring, and tentatively
commence writing again. I didn't discuss the details of her treatment
with her but I knew she had tried different medication, exercise and
modifications to her diet. She was wary of medicating herself into
complete mood stability because she then found she couldn't write,
and she was convinced that her mood was dictated by the seasons, a
particularly brutal kind of Seasonal Affective Disorder.

She talked and wrote about her death a lot, mostly cheerfully,
because when she was in communication mode she wasn't depressed.
She said she was 'someone to whom death just periodically draws near'
and that she had always been 'on a long piece of elastic from the
otherworld'. I hated her talking like this but it was clear that she was
reassured to think that, if the depression proved unbearable, she had
the means to free herself.

In 2004 Altán's beloved editor Philip left HarperCollins and Clare
Reihill took over. Clare was warm and supportive, she was passionate
about Altan's work and she acknowledged that, though the book was
taking longer to write than anticipated, it would be worth the wait.
Altán was still sending in new chapters but mostly she rewrote the
existing chapters or expanded her thoughts on the novel in her
handwritten letters to me. Her anxiety about how the material would
ever 'cut together' was mounting, and it wasn't unfounded. At the end
of 2004 she called me at home (I was on maternity leave) and asked
where the files relating to her work were kept. 'It's all stacked up in my

office,' I told her warily (no filing system would hold it by this time). 'Good. I'm coming to get it. I need to destroy the new stuff.' There was no dissuading her and by the time I returned to work, the stack was much diminished.

Over the next few years Clare and I waited. We encouraged and reassured Altán, met up with her and, from time to time, we lost touch. The mobile phone proved a huge boon. Altán rarely called but she would text, and that became her preferred method of communication. In August 2007, her mood began to slip. She was away but was writing a new chapter and was convinced that if she could get back home she would be able to continue working and pull herself out of depression. She sent me a frantic message:

> Georgia be prepared for a snowstorm of texts! I feel if I could get out of here and back to my work it would pull me back together! Talking to you activates the work bit of my mind. It is the strongest thing in my life. xxx

And, over the next few weeks, a 'snowstorm of texts' followed. They worried me and I wasn't sure how to respond but I recalled a friend, who'd recovered from a suicidal depression, telling me that simple confident statements, expressing the faith that he would get better – that he would feel different – had helped him. My replies throughout September and October amounted to just that, although I fretted that Altán would find them not so much simple as simple-minded. Increasingly anxious about her state of mind, I texted her. 'Can you recall what helps in this situation? I know you have felt like this before and then you have felt better.' She replied: 'Light. Otherwise it just seems to run its course. Spring light always fixes me.'

There were a few more texts; then, ominously, they petered out and in December 2007, with the winter solstice almost upon us, I got a call from a close friend of Altán's: the call I had so long been braced for, and so dreaded.

Two extracts from the early chapters of *Of Earthly Love* follow. They are not edited and are just as Altán first sent them to me. The first is the opening scene of the novel; the second is from chapter two – the events of which precede those of chapter one in the novel's chronology – and describes Blair and her mother's first encounter with Aoife, Blair's flatmate. In one of her early letters to me Altán said: 'I thought I would start with the funny and happy stuff in Dublin to get readers to step into my parlour, so to speak', and though she went on to wonder whether these opening pages were perhaps *too* light, she never seemed more satisfied with any of the revised beginnings that she wrote. So what follows is some of the 'funny and happy stuff': arch, playful, mock-heroic, blazing with intelligence and emotional truth, suffused with life and laughter. ■

FROM CHAPTER ONE

Richard and I sat up at night and agreed upon everything, except that my parents and I liked the *Irish Times* and he would not have it in the house. He sat in a chair at half one in the morning and read the English press.

And what a horrible, odious, rude and intolerable way of going on in the presence of a young woman, I thought: I am sitting here in quite the nicest nightdress, and any man with either sense or taste or manners would address himself to me.

And how dare he so comport himself, in fact, I thought, most pinstriped old sofa, most wicked old coal sack: for I am a very handsome girl, I thought, and accustomed to do what I like.

'I am totally bored,' I said. 'I am the enemy of newspapers. All the men I know are reading them ceaselessly at all times and they are a complete load of boys' fucking wank.'

'They are, actually,' Richard said, rather sadly, continuing to read furiously, as though it were not a nice habit at all, but one to which nature compelled. 'I am a boy.'

'I only like the *Irish Times*,' I said. 'And you never get it.'

'I will get it for you if you want it,' he said. He was not paying much attention. 'I just can't read it.'

He made a most interesting face.

'I can't read it in Dublin either,' I said. 'I only read it at home and on the train and on planes. I am actually not reading it all,' I said. 'It is just to stop horrible jerks talking to me. I have worked out a way of cracking it totally evilly at them, like a whip.'

I thought this would make him look up. It did not.

It is pointless, I thought: it is like beating the Hoover. His gaze continued to move over the page like a huge, semi-industrial German machine.

'The Brits are just hopeless,' he said, gloomily. He drew my attention to some acts of clownishness and meanness of spirit on the part of the London regime. 'Just fucking appalling.'

He spoke more in sorrow than in anger, I thought.

'Tories are lower than vermin,' I said, with energy. 'My father says that ceaselessly at all times, he is just madly in love with Nye Bevan. It is a pity we don't have them in the North,' I said. 'I am dying to open the door to one and just say that.'

'Well,' Richard said, spreading out the paper so that I could hardly see him and a tiny, annoying, paper spill was stuck in the delightful slow wheel of his voice. 'I'm just an old Whig, of course,' he said, turning over more pages.

'You are a horrible beast,' I said. 'You are doing to me what I do to the men on planes.'

'I'm sorry,' he said. He lowered the paper slightly and continued to read it. 'But these Tories are just disgusting.'

'I think they are vulgar as fuck as well,' I said. 'She is a vulgar woman. She is, in fact, totally mad,' I said. 'You can see it in her eyes.'

'Certainly mad to a degree which is not elegant,' Richard said, turning up his eyes in a quite perfect way, I thought, like a great courtesan simulating orgasm. He really has the best voice in Dublin, I thought: the voice of the medlars, heavy and espaliered, warm on the demesne wall.

'And the rest of them are just hopeless,' he said, sadly again. 'Except old Tarzan, he is a great man. Though she is the best, actually,' he said. 'What a monster.'

He continued to read the papers and oblige me to entertain myself by making interesting sounds in my mouth. I am throwing my voice back in my head, I thought, like a child bouncing a ball against a wall: just to pass the time, I thought, for he is not listening to me at all.

'*Quelle bande de cons,*' I said with great sensual enjoyment of the labial and nasal sounds. '*Elle, c'est une connasse.*'

'The Frogs were right, actually,' Richard said. 'The shopkeeper's daughter. Don't they love her?'

'I am madly in love with Napoleon,' I said. 'My mother and I are both deeply in love with him. I wouldn't go to bed with another Englishman if you paid me, in fact,' I said. 'They are so bad in bed it's not true, the most vulgar mixture you ever saw, of kind of kiddy and sado.'

'Well,' Richard said, a most repulsive grown-up nappy pinned lewdly over his voice. 'They've got Nanny now.'

'It is not Nanny,' I said. 'It is Matron. When I used to starch my shirts in college people just jacked off over me like mad.'

'Really?' he said. 'I wouldn't have.'

'That is because you can't smell anything and you don't fancy me anyway,' I said.

'You are wrong, actually,' he said.

'I am not wrong,' I said.

He was not looking at me.

'They got off on the smell,' I said, returning to thrash my subject. 'Turned them on like a fucking light switch, you never saw anything so disgusting in your life. You see this nightdress too, in fact,' I said. 'When I had it in college I had to not wear it to bed with people: it was either cut the sashes off or have them play horsey reins.'

'I like that nightdress,' he said. 'That is your nice nightdress.'

'I love it,' I said. 'I don't see why I shouldn't walk round in it all day, it is actually as well made as a dress. I am never dressed here anyway,' I said. 'Nobody cares.'

Richard was not listening to me. He was studying a picture of Mrs Thatcher, a strange lewd moistness seeping into his eyes.

And in the name of God, I thought, he is sitting there screwing a madwoman, and I simply never saw such a vile, vicious, depraved and degraded exhibition in my life. I bet he goes to the Bois de Boulogne, I thought, when he is in Paris, between brothels, and has sex there with deranged women and amputees. I would have sex with an ape first, I thought: I would strike off my right hand, I thought, before I would couch with a Tory, even Tarzan.

Perhaps, I thought, if I offer him some more wholesome pabulum, he will stop this quite vile feeding upon ordure.

'Come to bed with me,' I said. 'I am totally bored and it is the middle of the night.'

'I will come to bed,' Richard said.

'You won't,' I said. 'You say yes to everything and never do any of it.'

'Well, you know,' he said, spreading his palms and his voice in delightful mock-Jewry. 'Barristers. We have to.'

You horrible, horrible wicked beast, I thought: you only have use for me for the couple of moments it takes to caress the dog's ears, and then only if it puts its head in your lap.

'Well, I am going to go to bed,' I said. 'And then you will come and get into bed horribly an hour later and wake me up and I will never sleep again. And I hate having sex at two-thirty,' I said. 'When I am exhausted and you are completely drunk.'

'I will creep in like a coward,' he said.

'You will come like a thief in the night,' I could not prevent St John the Divine from saying in my voice. Richard laughed without looking up at the voice of Revelation, but ignored the call to repent.

It was clear to me he would continue for some time to luxuriate amid the blossoms of his sins, and then entirely fail to creep to bed.

'You will wake me up in any event,' I said. 'You walking about and breathing in the same room as me invariably wakes me up.'

'The princess and the pea,' he said, fondly and sadly, without looking up.

'It is called *The Real Princess*,' I said. 'I am the real princess. I don't feel you realize that at all.'

'I do, actually,' he said, concealing a gavial smile. 'I will come to bed. I am just going to do one more bit of law.'

'I will read a book,' I said. 'I may as well read your books,' I said. 'Since you just buy them and leave them sitting about.'

I took up a pretentious French book and went out of the room, raking cross nails through his hair as I passed. What appallingly wicked hair he has, I thought: a nasty dry lawn full of moss. But Catholics can never do grass, I thought, and, in fact, no one down here understands it except the horrible cricketers across the road: evil, emulous West Brits.

I got into Richard's bed and read the first pages of the book over and over again and could not understand a word, and it seemed to me that Richard was only able to read such works because of the peculiar denseness and dryness of his hair, which was generated by the character of his thought. It seemed to me that if I read any more I would cause my subtle emanation to migrate away from its task of making lustre in my own hair and skin, and Richard would never come to bed with me at all.

I placed the book on a pile of similar books covered thickly with dust, and tried to cause Richard to ascend the stairs by thought.

I caused my subtle emanation to descend the stairs and pull and tug at Richard as one pulls and tugs at one's mother's hand, I thought, when one is five years old, but Richard ignored it as completely as one's mother, when she continues talking, and pats one's head.

I curled up in a miserable Z. A smell *forte et dure* oppressed me.

What an appalling stench I thought: I never saw sheets their like. Richard's sheets had not been changed for so long they had acquired a sepia tint, and were covered in white spots and hairs, like an early film.

Downstairs he began to type.

The typing then ceased after an opening bombardment which I deduced had dispatched the legal matter, and I hoped for some moments Richard might come upstairs, but instead heard his evil feet bound down the stairs to the kitchen in a cheerful and surprisingly springy way.

A moment later I heard the pop of a cork.

The pounding of Richard's ancient electric typewriter then began again, its rhythm subtly altering to become both heavier and more fluent. From time to time it would cease for an interval, during which I knew Richard to remove the sheet of expensive laid paper on which he had typed only a few lines and throw it in the bin.

He had begun to type and revise the many vulgarly orotund paragraphs which composed a work on C. S. Parnell.

And it seemed to me I never heard anything more irritating in my life. It seemed to me that the writing of this work was the most revolting private nocturnal habit which could possibly be imagined in a man. It seemed to me I never heard of any production of vanity greater than the writing of private works of history by members of the Bar, nor any act of unnature more repulsive than a large and carnal barrister with a young woman in his bed who preferred to run the dust of ages through his fingers than caress the living flesh.

Every morning a disgusting wadded mass of Ciceronian periods lay discarded in the bin, their writing having detained Richard half the night. I knew he would now remain downstairs a considerable space of time, as when one's mother has met her favourite gossip, and will talk an hour.

I got up miserably and walked about.

Richard's evil bedroom seemed to me the most cheerless on earth.

Thin, whey-coloured light came through broken shutters and illuminated shirts floating sourly on the floor, like curds. I picked them up and placed them in the large new canvas laundry bin which Richard had bought and kept standing empty in the middle of the room, as savages display a commode. The large canvas laundry bin suddenly seemed to me to stand in the middle of the room in an unpropitious way: thirsty as a well unappeased by ritual clouts, and hungry as a standing stone.

It suddenly seemed to me that evil was near.

Evil is near me now, I thought, in this imperfect and malodorous shade: evil fawns and gambols, as the wicked weasel and the stoat. It is a great mistake to think evil is far, I thought, for evil is ever near: evil comes closer and closer, and soon will spring out, and pounce.

Evil suddenly twitched a wicked black-tipped tail from an orange bag in which Richard had bought a tie, whose black corded and tasselled handles seemed to me the most inauspicious thing I ever saw in my life. Death, death, death, I thought: the horses wear mourning cords. I am going down there now, I thought, and I will slay Charles Stewart Parnell.

I went down the stairs past the many little mandarins of descending

.

size which Richard kept on the landing windowsill, and found him sitting surrounded by thick blue smoke.

He did not even appear to notice as I approached him. I tried to let some air in by dragging spikes across his head.

'Ah,' he said. He wreathed a thick white sleeve around my hip. 'Blair.'

I continued to scarify his head.

'Your hair is appalling,' I said crossly. 'It is like podzol. The colour is totally leaching out of it,' I said. 'You must apply a million chemicals.'

'What's podzol?' Richard said with interest, not looking round.

I twanged his violet braces crossly.

'You are podzol,' I said. 'It is evil Russian soil that all the good has drained right out of, that is turning into evil ash.'

He laughed evilly. I took up a handful of evil hair and tried to tug it from an acid soil. 'Come to bed with me,' I said. 'I am miserable up there. Everything is frightening and your sheets are so disgusting it's not true.'

'What's frightening?' he said. He caressed my satin bottom. 'It's not frightening.'

'There is a frightening black tassel on an orange bag,' I said. 'Your laundry bin is witness to a past of unspeakable rites. The whole ghastly ensemble would scare anyone to death,' I said. 'I have taken fright.'

Richard swung the chair round to me and looked up with a deep and silent mineral laugh.

What strange and beautiful eyes he has, I thought: all the laughs and tears of the minerals: half the jewel and half the mine, I thought: great shade which has no name.

'What are you doing?' I said.

'Just some history,' he said.

'I suspected you of history,' I said.

I licked some beads of mourning nationalism from his forehead. It really doesn't taste of salt, I thought: he is made of jet and ash.

'You only sweat when you are doing history,' I said. 'You never sweat for law.'

'That's interesting,' he said. 'Is that true?'

'Yes,' I said. I sniffed him fondly. 'You smell completely disgusting. The cigars are the only good bit. It is absolutely foul in all other respects,' I said. 'It is the semen of wild boars.'

'Boars are good things,' Richard said, with deliberation.

'Wicked old things truffling about for filth,' I said. 'Truffling about in forests in French places.'

The name of the Fifth Republic called forth a further fond caress.

'I must just do one bit of law,' he said. 'Then I will come up.'

It is pointless, I thought: one might as well pet a gun carriage. But after a few minutes he did come up and tossed all his clothes on the floor.

He got into bed.

I put my cheek into a warm and foul declivity: there is another invisible one, just the same, on his back, I thought, where he hides the leathern wing.

'I was just doing a fee-note,' he said. 'I had to do it.'

'Like loading the dishwasher,' I said.

'Exactly like that,' he said.

A fond claw squeezed my arm.

Next morning he ran a hot iron over only the front of his shirt in a most un-Protestant fashion: they really are the most slack, idle, deceiving, unmilitary crew down here, I thought. I told him how ghastly he was in bed.

'You are completely fiendlike in bed,' I said. 'You are the most wicked old sofa. It is like lying under a horsehair sofa someone is jumping on.'

'Am I?' he said, with interest, a wicked apron of pleasure spreading leatherily across his face. He considers making love to women to be simply quite wrong, I thought: like wearing brown shoes to court. Slackness might occasionally tempt one to it, *mais vraiment, ça se fait pas.*

'Well,' I said. 'It is not entirely disagreeable. It is completely unique to you. I want to lie in bed all day, though,' I said. 'You never do.'

'Hours of dolphin-like caresses,' he said. 'I can't do that.'

How interesting, I thought: it is the same face he makes at the *Irish Times*.

'No,' I said. 'It is girls you want to do that with. The man you really want to go to bed with is a girl.'

Richard was not listening to me.

It is trousers, I thought: they are the splicing block of Eisenstein: as soon as they put them back on, I thought, the scene with the baby carriage is cut.

Richard rapidly put on his collar and tie and put in his links and studs.

'Well,' he said, entirely pleasantly, putting his coat on too. 'I'm off.'

He is pleased to be going, I thought, but he is pleased that I am here. He does like me really, I thought: it is just that I love him.

'Goodbye,' I said formally.

'I might see you later,' Richard said, pleasantly, walking over to the door. His tone twitches in just the sweetest way at that vulgarity, I thought: the most well-bred rabbit's nose. It is the only lacuna in his manners, in fact, I thought, but they are all the same down here: peasants, peasants, peasants, I thought: why can't they say goodbye?

'No,' I said. 'I will be gone.'

He turned back and ran up the bed in wonderful Russian bear-like fashion to give me a four-footed kiss.

'Goodbye, Blair,' he said, in quite the nicest way.

I caressed his delightful evil head. He is the only elegant man of his race, I thought: I love him now for good.

'Your tie is good with your scalp,' I said. 'Your scalp is the best bit of you, actually. It is the loveliest, spookiest blue, and kind of erectile.'

Richard laughed evilly and thundered off down the stairs, whistling some fragment, I thought, of Verdi.

FROM CHAPTER TWO

I too had liked the look of Aoife as soon as I saw her. She was a dark and clever-looking girl, older and bigger than me, who came down to meet us in the street and smiled and shook hands with us both in a peculiarly charming way, lively, but not casual to two strangers who had come a long way, and brought us up to the flat and invited us into a delightful smell of boiling stock and wine. She chatted fluently to my mother, to whom she had spoken on the phone, while I observed her covertly, and considered her one of the most distinctively attractive young women I had seen in a long time: like a longship, I thought, constructed of both strong female planks and spells, in the expectation she would last a hundred years.

Aoife and my mother liked one another too, I could see, in the way of tall women, and viewed one another as two high, carved heads first nod to one another, I thought, in the harbour, and then look at one another politely sidelong out of painted eyes and silver masks, and see with great joy they are two craft of the same shipwright, differing only in small ways. How happily then they bob at anchor, I thought: how merrily the waves speak their thoughts: how fervently they hope, and indeed, know in long bones that their meeting unties a lucky wind.

Aoife and my mother indeed resembled one another perceptibly apart from the darkness of Aoife's hair and eyes, and wore exactly the same amount of make-up and jewellery, I observed, though less make-up and more jewellery than me.

Aoife too was herself a solicitor.

My mother stood and contemplated Aoife against her background of a very clean and well-arranged flat together for a moment, as the last card in patience, I thought, finally got out, or the last knot untied in the witch's tarred string, so we could finally make some way.

'Now, isn't that just a lucky thing?' my mother said, as though aloud to the unseen hands who had helped it all along. 'Aoife could maybe help you with your study, if she has time some evening,' she said to me in her irritating schoolteacher's way of gently reproving by hortation.

'I must tell you, Aoife,' she continued, turning back to Aoife and uttering the name again with the particular pleasure of a person who has learned Irish later in life. 'You have a lovely name. Do you know how to spell Aoife's lovely name, Blair?' my mother said to me of Aoife's lovely name, which was pronounced like 'Eva' with an 'f'. 'It is AOIFE, like Aoine, Friday, that's a word you know,' my mother said, never missing an opportunity to implant in my mind some word of the Irish language. 'Aoine means a fast, or a scarceness as well,' she said. 'Of course that's a traditional thing on a Friday in the Catholic Church.'

I observed the correct deduction from this remark that we were Protestants enter Aoife's mind as neatly and silently as the otter dives: bright water barely marked with a splash. 'But Aoife was a daughter of the High King,' my mother said. 'It's a princess's name.'

'Blair is a lovely name too,' Aoife said politely to both of us, and part addressing me for the first time. 'Very unusual.'

'I named Blair after the loveliest girl I did my teacher training with,' my mother said, beginning to narrate in order to give Aoife and me an opportunity to look at one another. 'She was just a lovely person, from the Mourne direction, and lovely looking, like a princess. She married a minister and they went out as missionaries to Africa. I couldn't get a name for Blair, and then one day just as the six weeks you had to register were up, I remembered that girl I had chummed with, and so that was the name we had. The two of you could be like two princesses,' my mother concluded in the same irritating infants' school fashion, yoking Aoife and myself together by a single equally divided smile, as though setting us to share a desk.

It seemed a settled thing at once that I would rent the flat if that was agreeable to its owner, a businessman in Aoife's home town, she told us, for whose children she had babysat for years. Oliver, she told us too, was rarely in Dublin, though he kept a room for himself, but if he ever used it, he came in late and left early: sometimes she did not see him for months. The truth was, Aoife said, he left the flat largely to her, and she herself had the power to select as co-tenant a professional girl with whom she would get along.

'Well, you know, I think you two girls would get on the very best,' my mother said, as Aoife insisted on giving us a lunch of risotto she was making for herself since we had driven all the way from the North, after my mother had insisted for some time that we could not think of troubling her, and Aoife had overborne this resistance in a perfectly judged way, I thought, every grain of it delightfully coated in butter, but nonetheless palpably firm.

'Sure it's only a bit of old water and rice,' she said dismissively of her perfect risotto, adding a final ladle of boiling stock we could tell was home-made, and rapidly grating several further ounces of Parmesan with a small flat grater particularly adapted for that purpose which she had taken from a picture nail on the wall next to a similarly suspended grater, of larger size.

'I see you're a great cook, Aoife,' my mother said, addressing her by name again in a pleasant and deliberate way, as a mark of attention, as though to a new pupil on her first day, and looking around Aoife's kitchen full of jars and herbs and things hung up in clever ways. 'This young lady likes to cook too,' she said of me, as she had spoken of me to assistants in shops when I was fifteen. 'She learned to make lovely food one year from some Swiss people she lived with. You could make each other great meals.'

'We could surely,' Aoife said, with a smile to me which indicated to me she would like me to share the flat. 'We could keep each other well fed.'

'This young lady needs to eat her food,' my mother said, in the same fashion compounded of strong encouragement and mild reproof.

My parents had thought I had come home from Brussels very thin. 'Isn't that half the battle?' Aoife said. 'You need to eat.'

'Do you hear that?' my mother said to me, as though Aoife were not present, as she had told me as a child that friends' children loved their school uniforms and coats with hoods. 'You need to eat a breakfast, and you need carbohydrate, to give you energy. A rice dish is a very good thing for you to eat. I am glad to meet a girl, Aoife,' she said to Aoife, 'with the sense to cook herself a good meal.'

Then my mother talked solidly to Aoife for an hour and a half about places in the west where Aoife came from and my mother had driven round looking for native speakers with me in the car as a child, referring to all the places by their Irish names and adding their translations and places they were mentioned in the *Annals of the Four Masters* and the *Táin*, before moving on to Aoife's complete educational and legal careers, and the names and ages of her family.

'Isn't it a pity we never ran into any of you people one of those years we were down that direction?' my mother said. 'We were through all those towns several times and I met people in all of them. I just fell in love with that part of the world,' my mother continued, fondly. 'I would stop somebody along the road to ask the way, and since it was the Gaeltacht, you know, I would always greet the people in Irish. I would sometimes think maybe people didn't want to be bothered with it, but then I would think maybe people like to hear their own language spoken, and I would just say some simple little thing to whoever I met.'

She uttered some words in Irish to Aoife.

'I've forgotten all the Irish we did for Leaving Cert, I'm afraid,' Aoife said. 'It went in one ear and out the other.'

'Not at all!' my mother said. 'If you were brought up with a language round you, you'll always have it in your mind, like a tune in your fingers on the piano. Blair knows lots of Irish, she just doesn't realize it. I was learning my Irish when she was a child and I used to say my poetry when I was doing my housework.'

'*Ann-ya, ann-ya,*' I said, in an irritating moaning way. 'It was all exactly the same and totally miserable sounding.'

'That's just because you were a child,' my mother said, with her nearest approach to scorn. 'That was lovely poetry you were listening to. It's a wonderful language, a whole different world. You have to keep up your Irish, Aoife.'

She uttered some more words in Irish, and caused Aoife this time to laugh and reply.

'*Maith thu!*' my mother cried, with the first of her old brilliant smiles I had seen in a long time. 'What did I tell you?' She looked happily, and I thought, fondly at Aoife, as though at a pupil she knew would go far. 'They're great Irish speakers in your part of the world,' she continued. 'I would just say something to somebody along the road, and the next thing they would invite you up some wee country road to meet their mother or their father, or their sister or somebody, and next minute the whole family and all their neighbours would come in, and they would sing and play music and keep you all night and you wouldn't hear a word of English spoken. I'm going to speak Irish to you every time I come down,' my mother said to Aoife. 'If some lovely fellow hasn't come and spirited you away.'

Aoife blushed becomingly as my mother's eyes moved to the ring on her left hand.

'When are you getting married?' my mother said, smiling again, with a directness I could see Aoife thinking was a Northern thing.

'Oh,' Aoife said, blushing further. 'There's nothing like that arranged. We've known each other a long time, and he just kind of gave me a present of that last Christmas,' she said, with a glance notable for brevity, I thought, at the ring. 'It started off on the other hand for the first while,' she said. 'It kind of goes back and forth.'

'Well, any man doesn't marry you quick is a fool,' my mother said, dispositively. 'A lovely looking, clever girl, and a great Irish speaker, and a great cook. If he has any brothers, get one for this girl here,' my mother said, laughing happily as she got up, in a very irritating agricultural way. 'I'll let you find her a lovely boy.'

My mother arose, thanking Aoife for the lovely lunch with a beaming smile and pretended to spend some minutes in the bathroom redoing her hair and then looking at the rest of the flat and opening and closing the cupboards and looking out of the window in the room that would be mine, humming loudly to herself to let us know she was not listening, to allow Aoife and I to agree privately we would like to share the flat.

We reached an outline agreement immediately.

'Well,' Aoife said, with a delightful frank smile. 'I think your mother's right. I think the two of us would get on fine.'

'I think that too,' I said. 'I can always tell that instantly about people.'

'There's just one thing,' Aoife said, in an undertone, keeping her eyes fixed on the open door into the hallway, where my mother was exclaiming happily to herself on the largeness and commodiousness of the airing cupboard, and the unexpectedness of meeting with an airing cupboard in a modern flat. 'Oliver kind of uses this place more, like, to socialize than for work, that's why he doesn't look for a lot of rent. Not that he brings anyone back here, apart from his friends the odd time they're too cut to drive,' Aoife said, seeing at once which way my thoughts had turned.

'He comes up to Dublin basically to go out on his own, the odd time without his wife, if you see what I mean,' she explained. 'He has a few friends and they just go out and get drunk and buy drinks for the poor unfortunate girls working in clubs who have to put up with them. That's all it is, I'd say,' Aoife said. 'They think it's the high life. But sometimes if he comes in at night you're best to stay out of his way. I've never had any bother with him and in the morning he's up and off, that's one thing about Oliver, he's not one for lying in bed. I wouldn't say anything about it, though, to his wife, the odd time she'll come up to get clothes for her holidays or something. Not that she ever asks anything, she doesn't think that way,' Aoife said. 'Oliver never says anything either if I have anybody staying here, or anything like that.'

A very attractive dark directness in Aoife's gaze indicated that gentleman visitors were received, and I indicated that I could adapt myself to these parameters, and the next day she telephoned us to say that Oliver had no objection to anyone she was happy with, and a law student and everything, and shortly afterwards my mother brought me back with my possessions to move in. ∎

FAITH OF OUR FATHERS

Once at the heart of Irish life,
the Catholic priesthood faces
an uncertain future

Maurice Walsh

Gdansk, Poland. June 3, 1989. A moment of history on one of those damp, chilly summer evenings when the light seems to change with the wind. The Poles are on the eve of voting the Communists out of power and I am here with an Irish film crew to watch it happen. We find ourselves at a party in Lech Walesa's house on a tree-lined street somewhere on the edge of the city or certainly a journey away from the Germanic red-brick buildings at its centre. I don't remember much about the house except that it seemed very modern in a Scandinavian way with lots of wooden cladding; I recall thinking at the time that Walesa must have built or renovated it with the money from his decade of fame. From speakers somewhere upstairs Whitney Houston was blasting out 'I Wanna Dance with Somebody' to the whole neighbourhood. We had driven there in our hired Polish car (like a punchline from some Iron Curtain joke, the knob on the gearstick had come off).

All over the city there was a great sense of anticipation and the streets seemed to be emptying out. The following day Poland would be the first Warsaw Pact country to have the opportunity to get rid of the Communist Party. The agreement to have a free election might go wrong; they might seize the ballot boxes at the last minute. The only reason we had gained access to Walesa's house was because the director of our film was an Irish priest, Father Joseph Dunn, a man well known in Ireland for his television documentary series *Radharc*, a Gaelic word meaning vision. In nearly thirty years as a film-maker, Joe had drawn on a network of contacts in the Catholic Church throughout the world and he came to Poland with an introduction to the parish priest of Gdansk, who also happened to be Walesa's confessor.

In Poland our base was a seminary in the middle of Warsaw, which saved Joe money. It was strange at first to be there in a little room with a desk and a hard bed, to feel like a student preparing for a theology lecture and then to go to lunch in a communal refectory. But I could see the attractions of a regulated life in pleasant surroundings and, being both Irish and Catholic (though by then lapsed), it didn't seem unnatural to be working with a priest and staying in a such a place.

That Saturday we left Warsaw early and drove to Gdansk. All the interviews we did that day were merely a prelude to the evening at Walesa's house. We all knew him as the electrician in the donkey jacket who had organized the strikes in the shipyards in 1980, but there he was in a check suit, plump and small, almost passing for a member of the gentry, smiling and clinking his vodka glass with his guests. Ham, chicken, beef, gherkins and cucumber salad were laid out on tables in the kitchen and luminaries of Solidarity picked at the food. Adam Michnik, who only a few years previously had been imprisoned under martial law for 'attempting to overthrow socialism' (and who had written a book about how Solidarity and the Catholic Church could be allies), waved his glass in a noisy toast. A wealthy American woman in a white dress who was interested in buying the shipyards at Gdansk edged forward to be introduced, her corporate lawyers hovering uneasily behind her. John Tusa, then Managing Director of the BBC World Service, presented Walesa with a bottle of cognac and then

Father Joseph Dunn, founder and director of Radharc Films

mixed with the rest of us. When he was introduced to Joe, Tusa eyed his Roman collar in disbelief. 'That's not real, is it?' he said with mock British disdain (or at least we hoped it was mock disdain). Joe fingered his collar and smiled shyly.

As we stood drinking wine we heard shouts and the blare of car horns from the street outside. A procession of Solidarity supporters was driving up and down past Walesa's house to salute him on the eve of what was expected to be a great victory. Joe picked up his camera from the floor and set off to film the celebration, while Walesa went out to his front gate to receive the acclamation. Many of his guests followed. On the footpath I found myself alongside Tusa again, who leaned towards me to be heard above the din. 'Where's Father Eisenstein gone?' he asked. I pointed to Joe, a slim figure in his grey jumper and trousers, down on one knee with the camera on his shoulder and turning to follow the cars with their fluttering banners and flags.

Joe Dunn was one of twenty-two priests ordained at Clonliffe College in Dublin in 1955. At that time there were eight major seminaries throughout Ireland and, including the houses of formation for religious orders, there were some 4,000 students preparing to be priests and brothers. In 2007 two priests were ordained in the whole of Ireland. Last year thirty men entered the two remaining seminaries.

Each year the number of new priests ordained is a fraction of the number of old priests who die. Some estimates say that in twenty years there will be only 1,500 priests left in Ireland. When Joe Dunn left the seminary in the mid-Fifties, foreign visitors would remark on how many priests you would see in a normal day walking through Dublin. In a memoir written a few years before his death in 1996 Joe remembered Clonliffe as dull and claustrophobic and vented a raw irritation about having to wear a stupid wide hat and being forbidden to go to the theatre or read the newspapers. But life was about to change for Joe and for Ireland.

After television arrived in our house in 1965, my mother would often tell us to be quiet if a priest came on. It rarely mattered what he was saying; it was worthy of our attention because he was a priest and he was talking and therefore, just as you might defer to him if he was standing right there in the kitchen, you needed to pay heed to his voice even though it was coming out of the television. The association 'priest/talking' took shape in my head. But in the late 1960s, there were some priests who seemed to have more interesting things to say than those who caused us to be interrupted and ordered to listen to their ramblings.

One of these was Father Joe Dunn. When *Radharc* came on we often watched it without being told to pay attention. It was sometimes a documentary from abroad – perhaps a Latin American country where Irish missionaries were helping the poor, or coverage of the Biafran War in Nigeria – but even when it was about Ireland the stories *Radharc* was telling and its black-and-white footage made familiar landscapes a little bit strange. Joe's nasal, middle-class Dublin voice would occasionally narrate a script and sometimes he'd appear himself in black coat and collar to introduce a film. The programmes were never overtly radical but, particularly when they examined religious themes abroad, they revealed a world filled with debate and in which Christian lives were rarely as tranquil as they appeared immediately beyond our kitchen. After Joe's death, Peter Kelly, who worked with him for many years and had been at Lech Walesa's party in Gdansk, wrote that Joe had often spoken of how he saw his foreign films about religious issues as parables for what could be happening in Ireland.

Every Sunday and every holy day we cycled to Mass in the village three miles away. I can still smell the cold, brown varnish from when I knelt down and pushed my nose against the top of the front pew, and hear the shrill tinkle of the altar boy's bell as the priest raised the chalice. Great changes to the liturgy hatched at the Second Vatican Council between 1962 and 1965 were being gradually introduced. One Sunday, instead of the priest intoning the Latin Mass with his back to the congregation ('yapping away at the wall', as an irreverent teacher used to describe it to us), he stood at a temporary altar facing us. A new Mass book in English was handed out and I remember people examining it in wonder: a familiar, opaque ceremony made strange by its new plainness and thrust into their lives from afar.

For all our religiosity it seems curious now that priests were really quite distant and it was unusual to have direct contact with them. When we were preparing for Communion in the local village school, Father Smith came into our classroom and drew a random series of *x*s on the green blackboard, the sleeves of his black coat shiny and rustling. The *x*, he told us, was a sin. When we went to confession God would forgive us and – he took the duster and wiped out all the *x*s – our sins would be erased.

I can hardly remember a priest coming to our house except on one occasion when we hosted a Station, a custom dating from the seventeenth century when, because of a shortage of churches, the priest celebrated Mass in the houses of his parishioners. In our house on the night before the Station, the parlour, a room never frequented except at Christmas, with a pristine couch and armchairs, a carpet and a polished table, was prepared for breakfast. The table was moved to the middle of the room, a lace tablecloth draped on it and then laid with the best china. Butter pats were rolled with two butter curlers, leaving a little pile of coiled, striated, melting butter. On the morning of the Mass, respectable people from the parish were invited to join the priest for a fried breakfast in the parlour, a rare treat. Excluded from the room until the guests had started to leave, I rushed in to examine what they had left behind and went from plate to plate picking up bacon rinds and dangling them into my mouth.

In 1950 almost 8,000 people took part in a pilgrimage to Knock, the shrine in County Mayo, on one August day. Everywhere you look on the pages of Irish newspapers during that decade there is religion and bishops and priests exhorting and warning and pronouncing about how people should live their lives. In April 1952 the Bishop of Meath cautioned people in the Midlands to beware when in the town of Tullamore: it was 'a far cry from the days when it was a village' (and therefore of no danger to good Catholics) and in growing had provided 'a greater occasion of sin for the young people'. That same year the Papal Nuncio visited Mount St Joseph Abbey in Roscrea, County Tipperary, and described Ireland as 'a regular oasis' in a world where communism was rampant.

I once had reason to look something up in the *Sunday Press* of August 15, 1954. When the newspaper was brought to me in the library, I was struck by the huge headline on the front page: IRISH THRONG LOURDES FOR A GREAT MARIAN CLIMAX.

> From Kevin Devlin, *Sunday Press* reporter in Lourdes.
>
> Fervently demonstrating their Faith, Irish pilgrims prayed late into the night and the early hours of yesterday morning at the Grotto here as the Feast of the Assumption brought the climax to the Marian Year in Lourdes.
>
> And yesterday, with banners flying, the Irish marched through the streets of the town to the official opening of their pilgrimage at 10 a.m. when the Archbishop of Dublin, Most Rev. Dr McQuaid, delivered the opening address.

Even by the late 1960s and early 1970s, the idea that Irish people praying late into the night at a shrine in France should be worthy of this kind of attention would have seemed quaint. The great surge in the power of the Catholic Church in Ireland, which had gathered strength after the Famine in the mid-nineteenth century, was slackening as the country became richer. Piety was slowly dissolving and jeremiads from bishops about keeping bad company and nudity in theatres were laughed off. While Joe Dunn was working behind the camera, a new generation of clergy had become personalities on television. Some, like Eamonn Casey, the fast-talking, hearty Bishop of Kerry, and Father Michael Cleary, a priest who played his guitar and sang ballads, were gifted with showmanship and greedy for attention; others, like Father Fergal O'Connor, a lecturer in Politics at University College Dublin, were prepared for argument. Father O'Connor often appeared on *The Late Late Show*, a live chat show on Saturday nights which aired debates on previously forbidden topics and provoked rows in families between parents and their children, who wanted to stay up to watch. Father O'Connor was in favour of abolishing mandatory celibacy, of ordaining women priests and introducing divorce.

By the late 1970s I had become one of the editors of the school magazine at the Christian Brothers Secondary School in Carrick-on-Suir. We were all in favour of glasnost in Catholic Ireland. We also had a very enlightened teacher who was prepared to drive us around the country to conduct interviews with prominent people and one cold, dank February day three of us from the fifth year went to interview Father O'Connor in his presbytery in a rundown part of Dublin. I remember him as a short, beak-nosed man whose hands were twisted by arthritis. He spoke gently and encouragingly. Our questions were invitations for the sanctions we wanted to hear: should women be ordained? Should priests be allowed to marry? Should divorce be allowed? We asked him about contraceptives. They were permissible, he said, if without them the meaning of marriage would be damaged. But he added that contraceptive lovemaking was always 'a lesser thing' and was, as such, imperfect.

Around this time I was friendly with an older boy from the class above me. We used to talk about religion and politics on the yellow school bus during the forty-five-minute journey home. In his final year in school he discovered that he had a vocation and suddenly joined a religious order that had its origins in Mexico called the Legionaries of Christ. The following year he invited me to an open day at the order's headquarters in Dublin and I decided to go. I didn't really feel I wanted to be a priest or a brother but I thought it would be interesting to meet these people: I expected them to be open-minded, that our conversations would be similar to the chats Philip and I used to have on the bus, and among the books I packed for my few days in the seminary were *The Communist Manifesto* and Bertrand Russell's *Why I am Not a Christian.*

A few days after Christmas I arrived at the central bus station in Dublin. Weak January light flooded through the huge glass windows; it seemed a very big place to me. I was met by one of the brothers who drove me to the south of the city. I didn't talk to him much out of shyness and because I was excited by being in Dublin for only the third time in my life; I had never been to Foxrock before, but people from the country regarded it as one of the most well-appointed addresses in Dublin, a synonym for wealth and privilege. The headquarters of the order was in a building that seemed like a modern apartment block or a hotel, five or six storeys high. There was a crib in the foyer and a Christmas tree with beautifully wrapped presents laid out on the parquet floor underneath it in that perfect way you see in Christmas films set in New York. The whole place exuded well-heeled busyness and comfort.

There were three others like myself, all of us invited for a day or two to see if we might have vocations. It was explained to us that one of the aims of the order was to foster the emergence of a middle class in Latin America so as to bridge the gap between rich and poor and thereby prevent revolutions. We were introduced to some rich Mexican children and the understanding was that a lot of the good work towards killing off revolutions was being done with the money their fathers were giving to the order for their children to have a good time in Foxrock. One of their families had donated a video recorder to the recreation room and they played an Abba special over and over again. It was the first time I had ever seen a video recorder.

That evening I met my friend Philip, now wearing a long black soutane, and there was an elaborate opening of late Christmas gifts between him and the other brothers. They treated each other with a masculine bonhomie that was meant to show how confident and well-mannered they all were. After tea we were brought to a room where a brother told us we would watch a film about the life of Che Guevara. I can't remember what he said but I'm sure the idea was that we would be inoculated against revolutionary violence. The lights were turned down and the projector screen lit up in Technicolor; Omar Sharif played Che Guevara and Jack Palance was Fidel Castro. As I watched Sharif succumb to another asthma attack during a battle in the bush and then fight on after lying down to take a few puffs from his inhaler, my interest in Che and revolution soared.

That night the three potential postulants gathered together in one bedroom after lights out. The other two were smoking and were clearly less interested than I was in what the Legionaries of Christ might be about to do in Latin America. Neither of them seemed blessed with a vocation. From the window we looked out across the shimmering lights of the distant city. It was too late to search for the toilet in the darkened corridors so the one with the curly hair pissed into the sink and we spluttered with repressed laughter as we turned on the taps and washed it away. At breakfast the following morning, a discussion began about the Che Guevara film. At one stage I said something about there being good socialists and a brother turned to me and said, 'There are no good socialists!'

Not long after this my friend Philip left the Legionaries of Christ and I went to college in Dublin. I didn't know anybody who was training to be a priest. In September 1979 Pope John Paul II came to Ireland and for three days we were all transfixed, watching his helicopter on television appear out of the sky above thousands of people waving their flags and hankies. Bishop Eamonn Casey and Father Michael Cleary, 'the singing priest', did great warm-up turns at some of the venues, and I went to see the Pope in Limerick. Hundreds of thousands of people were standing on the racecourse waiting for him when the late September sun rose. Then the helicopter appeared. It was the last day of his visit and he delivered a hardline speech saying Ireland must remain a bastion of Catholicism in a secular world. I remember thinking that three young women drinking cans of lager near me would be sure to ignore him.

In the decade after the Pope left there were fierce battles over abortion and contraception and divorce, and the bishops and their lay allies seemed to have won most of them. Then one day in May 1992 people woke up to hear on the news that Bishop Eamonn Casey had left the country after admitting that he was the father of a seventeen-year-old boy who lived in America. A few years later, after Father Michael Cleary died, it emerged that he had a son too and that all the time he had been on the television and radio upholding the Church's teaching on sex he had been living with his housekeeper as if she was his wife. It was also around this time that the first cases of the sexual abuse of children by priests were heard in the courts.

There are more trains in the direction of Maynooth, in County Kildare, than ever before. Out here, to the west of Dublin, is the commuter land of the economic boom of the last decade, where stations have been built to service the new houses. Under the bright blue sky a big plastic banner bearing the words MOVE ON UP! hangs from a fourth-floor balcony of a new block of apartments between Ashtown and Phoenix Park. But all of these houses are rapidly losing their value so it might as well say MOVE ON OUT!

In my carriage a young woman in a red coat, returning to Sligo after making a presentation in Dublin, is on her mobile phone. She tells her friend she was asked what she would do if they cut €20,000 out of her budget. The Polish man pushing the tea trolley through the carriage recognizes her; they know each other from a hotel in Sligo where he used to work. He says he hears it's not doing very well these days; he's happier working on the train. As he dips her teabag in and out of her plastic cup, she calls her mother and asks, 'Is Prague lovely?'

We glide by the bare trees and the brown tilled fields, parallel with the canal, past a heron shaking its wings and three men in bright yellow jackets clearing weeds from the towpath with spades. There is a sign for Carton House, European Golf Resort of the Year in 2008. It was here that Princess Grace and Prince Rainier stayed when they visited St Patrick's College, Maynooth, in 1963. Founded in 1795, reportedly in order to keep Irish Catholics from imbibing French revolutionary ideas in seminaries on the Continent, Maynooth very quickly became the citadel of Irish Catholicism. It was the pre-eminent seminary, the intellectual centre of the Irish Church and the place where the bishops met to pronounce on the great issues of the day.

The experience of Maynooth evoked a powerful nostalgia in many of those who passed through it, analogous to the relationship between the British ruling class and Oxford. In a representative memoir written in the 1930s, a seminarian, Neil Kevin, suggested that putting Maynooth out of action would be the prime objective of any communist worth the name. Back in 1825 Daniel O'Connell, the Irish political leader who won Catholic emancipation from religious discrimination, once described priests who emerged from Maynooth as 'the children of exceedingly vulgar people', but by the end of the nineteenth century Maynooth graduates were the bright sons of strong farmers who knew they were being trained for a very privileged and powerful social position. Neil Kevin recalled the early-summer processions at the college in the 1920s to celebrate the Feast of Corpus Christi: 'the coloured capes of fifty priests, five hundred students in a slowly moving line of white, the tasselled banners of Our Lady and the saints; incense, flowers, and hymns in the open air.' He imagined a never-ending stream of priests leaving the college chapel and scattering across the earth, 'unbroken... ever renewing itself... and setting out again before the fathers and mothers of Ireland, whose eyes are dim at the sight of it.'

At Maynooth station many students leave the train but it is unlikely, these days, that any of them are seminarians. After a handful of lay students were first admitted to Maynooth in 1966 a secular university grew and has now swamped the seminary altogether. There are over 8,000 students at the National University of Ireland, Maynooth. When I reach the square of the old seminary after walking through the town that the clerical students were once forbidden to enter unless accompanied by a supervisor, I see young women with iPods on their way to lectures, but I see nobody in a black soutane. In the buildings around the square the rooms that were once dormitories for the seminarians are now offices of the university.

I have come to meet Father Michael Mullins, a lecturer in Sacred Scripture who hails from my hometown, Carrick-on-Suir. His room, where he has just finished a seminar, is like the study of an Oxford don, the sofa and armchairs strewn with books and papers. We are joined by one of his graduate students, Sean Corkery, who was one of two priests ordained last year.

Father Mullins recalled reading that someone had once described Ireland as being like a rather well-managed monastery. But he had been a student at Maynooth in the early 1960s, when many of the changes introduced by Vatican II began to take effect, and said he could sense even then that this state of affairs would not continue: the day was coming when Ireland would be much less devoted to religion. He even noted that there were troubled times ahead for the clergy in his first Mass after ordination, or, as he put it elliptically in his sermon that day, that the shadow of the cross would fall across the priests of Ireland. When he was in charge of vocations in County Waterford in the 1980s he could be sure of a good response in schools; pupils were still eager. Now, if he was in the same position, he would feel obliged to advance a kind of apologia for the priesthood. He professed to be quite enthused by the fact that priests can't assume their place in Ireland any more. From his reading of history he came to see the ebb and flow of the Church's fortunes as quite natural; the Church has been both powerful and marginal through the centuries. Periodically, he said, it would shed its skin like a snake. But then, almost as an afterthought, he added that he feared that a Church which could not produce replacement priests from among its own people was in trouble; that the steady decline in vocations represented a wearing away of the faith.

The story of Sean Corkery's vocation could hardly be more different from the special calling of the glorious days of vocations in Ireland. In his secondary school in Cork religion was regarded as a bit of a laugh by his fellow pupils. His family was religious and he had been an altar boy but later he drifted away from Catholicism, trained to be a chef and went off to work in Australia.

After he returned to Ireland in his early twenties, however, he found that he was still interested in the priesthood. He went to see the director of vocations in his own diocese and said, while confessing his desire to enter a seminary, 'I think I am mad.' The director of vocations agreed. And so at the age of twenty-four Sean Corkery entered Maynooth. He was ordained last year and is now studying Moral Theology as a postgraduate. At the end of next year he will be assigned a parish. He is taking nothing for granted; he says you can't make any assumptions about your parishioners any more, even whether they are married. Sean's ambition is minimalist: as a priest, you must live your own faith, and then you might be doing well to influence ten people.

They offered me a tour of the college. On the walls along the corridor outside Father Mullins's study we passed framed photos of each year's graduates. These are objects of special sentiment for men who have been to Maynooth. Members of each ordination class have their photos taken individually; then they are arranged by the photographer, with some decorative flourishes, in one big frame known as the class-piece. Every priest trained at Maynooth would have his own copy of the class-piece. The larger frames from the 1940s and 1950s are crammed with dozens of oval portraits of youthful faces, some in semi-profile, some with shy smiles. But as the years go by the number of photos in each frame diminishes and the photos themselves grow larger. Finally, the class-piece for 2007 consists of only four large photos, and two of these students had yet to be ordained when their portraits were taken.

As Sean explains it when he is describing how unfathomable his decision to enter the seminary appeared to his friends and acquaintances, priests are not a group you would want to be attached to. Since the child-abuse scandals, Father Mullins thinks that even parents are anxious about their sons becoming priests, as if it were a sign not of holiness but of potential depravity. Both priests are able to describe incidents of overt hostility. When Sean was a seminary student he was with friends in a nightclub back home in Cork when a guard came over and started berating him, asking what right a priest had to show his face in public. Two years ago Father Mullins was walking from an ordination ceremony to the reception along the seafront in Galway. As he passed a group of young children playing football a man rolled down the window of a passing car and shouted, 'Hey, you! Leave those children alone!' Once, on a social occasion, a man asked the company, in Father Mullins's presence, what the definition of the word 'priest' was. His answer: Paedophile Ring in Every Small Town.

The child-abuse scandals of the last fifteen years have permanently altered the relationship between the Church in Ireland and its people. Rather than being quick to protect children from abusive priests, the Hierarchy was revealed to be full of inept leaders who covered up what had happened, shielding priests from the consequences of their behaviour, dealing with victims and their families callously and thoughtlessly, more fearful of the public reputation of the Church than the damage done to devout believers. The opening frames of Mary Raftery's 2002 television documentary on the abuse cases in the Dublin diocese, *Cardinal Secrets*, show a series of Dublin churches shot from a helicopter, a view that renders them unfamiliar, like landmarks in another country, not the Catholic Ireland we knew. Cynically, many dioceses had taken out insurance policies to protect themselves from lawsuits well before the scandals broke while remaining evasive and defensive about what happened. In the last decade the moral authority of the Church has been so undermined that priests are no longer guaranteed a civil hearing in public. It used to be that priests chose not to wear their collars as a gesture of openness or because it was the fashion in Latin America. Now, they often go without them because they don't want to be recognized as priests.

The details of encounters between priests and their victims, recounted endlessly in newspaper reports of court cases as well as in official reports, were especially shocking to people accustomed to regarding their priests as holy men. As with abuse that occurs within families, a recurring feature of all these stories is the instinct of children not to tell about what went on because they did not expect to be believed. And indeed their parents often refused to believe or even to be worried by hints and rumours because it was simply impossible to entertain a thought that priests could abuse children. One of the reasons the notorious Father Sean Fortune – who committed suicide in 1999 at the start of his trial on sixty-six counts of sexual assault of boys – was able to get away with the outrageous abuse of his position for years was that people in his parish often supported him because they could not believe that a priest would lie.

The abuse scandals also revealed the extraordinary paradox of how, in an authoritarian church, priests seemed to be immune from sanction by their bishops. Bishop Brendan Comiskey, the central character in *The Ferns Report*, the judicial inquiry into clerical abuse of children in the Diocese of Ferns, in County Wexford, which was commissioned by the Irish Government in 2002 and written in lucid prose by a judge and two child protection specialists, emerged as a figure by turns tragic and taciturn, who knew very little about the priests in his diocese. He could go for months without seeing them and he certainly did not manage them in any sense. In fact, he often appeared to be afraid of them – of what they might do if he took action – to the extent that on occasion they responded to his inquiries with insolence. The priests seemed to live as they chose, with no accountability to anybody, least of all to their nominal superiors. But there was another side to this autonomy. The priest was often isolated from everybody, deferred to by his parishioners yet ignored by those superiors. Many priests had not been happy people for a long time.

In 1988, fewer than ten years after the rapturous welcome given to the Pope, the National Conference of Priests in Ireland met to discuss what priests should be doing with themselves. The published account of the priests' concerns is punctuated by words like 'uncertain', 'irrelevant', 'inadequate' and 'anxiety'. They were unsure of their role in a church that was supposed to devolve power to the laity and they felt themselves to be scapegoats for the increasing criticism of the Church in Ireland. 'Efforts are made to fill us with a sense of guilt for all the mistakes of the past,' one priest wrote (without any sense of irony about a priest protesting at being forcibly filled with a sense of guilt). Fundamentally, many priests thought of themselves as lesser people than their married friends, wondering if the disciplined life of the seminary had prepared them to be 'social eunuchs in a world that prizes encounter and intimacy'.

It is odd to read now of how these often brash and domineering men who denounced their opponents in the culture wars of the 1980s were themselves consumed with guilt and self-loathing. Their state of mind suggests that the malaise in the Irish Church long preceded the abuse scandals. Even the decline in vocations, only now being widely discussed, was trenchantly analysed in a report commissioned by the Irish bishops as far back as 1971, when a drop in the number of priests and nuns had been registered for the first time in the twentieth century. This report likened the popularity of vocations between the 1930s and 1950s to the stream of emigrants leaving impoverished Ireland for Britain and America, abandoning a pervasive sense of futility in search of better lives. A vocation could be seen, the report said, as another form of flight from the intolerability of life in Ireland. With the opening up of new economic possibilities in the 1960s, life did not seem so bad after all. Crucially, the report noted that as the number of pupils in secondary schools increased (free secondary education was introduced in 1968), vocations started to decline. For those who might once have considered entering seminaries or convents, new careers and universities now beckoned. Moreover, the report noted, 'love and sex and marriage [are] no longer painted with danger signs' and parents now wanted to see their children as 'good Christian lay people rather than doubtful priests and nuns'.

In 1965 Joe Dunn made a film about his old seminary, Clonliffe College. Joe introduced it – glancing down quickly as he spoke to the camera – as a foray behind the high-walled building that people might recognize from their walk to a football match in Croke Park. The opening shot is of an intense young preacher with high slicked-back hair and wild eyes filmed against a white background; he might be from an Orson Welles film of the 1940s. He is talking about vocations but you sense, as he glowers intimidatingly from side to side, that he is about to burst into condemnation. Suddenly he is interrupted by a gentle voice to his left: 'Oh wait, wait...' The camera pulls back to reveal that the young preacher is addressing five or six other clerical students sitting on chairs opposite him in a seminar room. He has been interrupted by his teacher. 'No advertiser and nobody in TV would start off with, "I would first give you a definition of a vocation." You need to find a story. How about St Paul?'

This little vignette announces that even a seminary – a mysterious place behind high walls – is now, in the mid-1960s, modern. The young preacher is being judged against the television and the advertisement. Subtly, Joe Dunn's film is bringing us face to face with the modern world that would overwhelm Irish Catholicism. There are shots of sports day when the seminarians unbutton their soutanes and don sweaters and polo shirts. Some of the close-ups could be from a fashion shoot. One handsome chiselled face poses pensively with a cigarette, fingers splayed and thumb twisting on front teeth. They walk down the street in Dublin to Mass in their long soutanes, wide-brimmed hats and gloves. For dramatic contrast the camera picks out posters for ballroom dances as they pass. They look most joyous of all when they put on their ties and hats and ride on their bicycles through the almost deserted streets to University College Dublin to take a course with lay students. One of them tells the camera that he much prefers coming here than having the lectures in Clonliffe because it is an escape from the atmosphere of the seminary. 'I'm sure it's the right system,' a very young seminarian says, and then laughs and shrugs. 'But there could be a lot of improvements, a lot of modernizing, because I don't think the seminary is preparing men at the moment...'

It is December 8 in Enniscorthy, County Wexford. A light rain is falling on the Feast of the Immaculate Conception. This used to be the day when country people would go to Mass and then to Dublin for a special shopping trip before Christmas. The night before I had flown into Dublin on the last flight out of Heathrow. It was full of people who had been visiting the stores in London; a woman squeezed past carrying a Harrods bag and a bottle of champagne. As I drove out of the airport it was nearly ten o'clock and from the radio the voice of a Ukrainian tenor filled the darkness of the car. The voices kept coming on the way to Enniscorthy: a traditional music show with hornpipes

Henri Cartier-Bresson's image of priests at a football match, Maynooth, 1962

and fiddles and a presenter who looked forward to next week *'le cúnamh Dé'* – with God's help. After the news (a man in his fifties shot dead in Dublin) there was the voice of Seán Óg Ó Ceallacháin, still on the radio after what must be fifty years, reading the weekend GAA results on a Sunday night: Roscommon senior football final, Louth intermediate camogie semi-final. With the wide roads and the new motorway I was in Enniscorthy in two and a half hours.

Even though it was nearly midnight there were several full tables in the bar of the hotel. A group of women in their sixties with Dublin accents were drinking pints at one table; across from me a plump, red-faced man was telling a story about having had a chain stolen from his neck in a bar in Miami. Someone else chipped in with an anecdote about a man who had phoned *The Gerry Ryan Show* about an incident that had happened in Istanbul. It was clear that the plump man assumed everything he said would be thought either hilarious or significant. Now he was telling them that although venison was supposed to be high in cholesterol, it was low fat. This led to a discussion of the best rifle to shoot a deer with. The plump man said the .308 was a powerful weapon – the Americans were shooting Muslims in Iraq with it from 1,700 yards away. And wasn't the last English soldier shot in the North killed with a .308?

The next morning there were no rashers or sausages for breakfast. The papers were full of news about how all Irish pork and bacon had been recalled because they had found traces of a deadly contaminant in pig feed. Processing factories were closing down and pig farmers were facing ruin.

I had chosen December 8 to spend with a priest because it had always been an important holy day. I had found Father Bill Cosgrave, whose parish was near Enniscorthy, through a friend who had shown me some articles Father Cosgrave had written about the current role of the priest. When I called him for directions Father Cosgrave said – a few times – that there would be a very poor crowd; people didn't turn up for church on holy days any more. Driving through the drizzle I veered left after I crossed the bridge and after O'Donoghue's garage took the road for Boolavogue, the village that appears in the famous ballad commemorating the local priest Father John Murphy, who was hanged for taking part in the 1798 rebellion.

It took ten minutes to arrive in the village of Monageer. The church and the priest's house are side by side. The church dates from 1870 and the priest's house itself was built in 1846, at the height of the famine. Father Bill Cosgrave is a slim sixty-seven-year-old man whose front room has the air of being the only room in the house he occupies. Along the wall inside the door are bookcases full of works on theology; near the window above his desk is a painting of a bishop who was his father's uncle. Father Cosgrave is getting ready to say the ten o'clock Mass. He chats for a little while and it is only at about ten to ten that he hurries me along. A few minutes later he is appearing on the altar.

A woman and two children had arrived early and begun to say the rosary with an older woman near the front of the church. Slowly people shuffled in to take their places in the simple pews – twenty of them lined up on either side of the church. By the time Father Cosgrave appeared on the altar with a girl and a boy to serve Mass there were forty-three adults and a baby in the church. I counted only eleven men, most of them elderly; there was one man in his twenties and only one teenage boy. There was little sense of occasion (few people seemed to have put on special clothes) and an overall feeling of duty and devotion. I was reminded of an expression Father Cosgrave used in an article for a theological magazine, when he wrote of how, unlike cults and sects, the Catholic Church did not expect its members to be 'religious *virtuosi*' striving for perfection, but required nothing more than 'a sort of mass standard of religious commitment', the kind of interest they might bring to membership of a football club. Clearly there had been a slump in the mass standard of commitment. Nonetheless when Father Cosgrave invited people to exchange a sign of peace during the Communion rite, my neighbours – an elderly man and two women – reached across with enthusiasm to shake hands with each other and with me, a stranger.

The theme of the Mass was set by the missal leaflet: 'Because Mary had such an important part to play in the plan of Salvation, God, in choosing her as the mother of his Son, preserved her from sin even from the moment of her conception.' In his sermon Father Cosgrave explained how the emphasis had shifted from Mary as a model of chastity to Mary as a model of faith. Chastity used to be perceived as the number one virtue, Father Cosgrave said, so that anything to do with sex was 'a bit dicey' and it was better to stay away from it. 'We still believe that she was a virgin of course...'

After Mass, when I was poring over the newspapers and leaflets in the church porch, I was struck by a notice pinned to the wall like a warning or a disclaimer. The POLICY NOTICE set out how the Church was committed to doing everything 'to create a safe environment for children'; if anything went wrong the reader was encouraged to call the mobile phone of a person described as the Parish Child Protection Rep. Despite the publicity given to the abuse scandals for several years, it was still a shock to be faced with this. It created the impression that the church inside, as well as being somewhere to pray, might be a risky place where you would need to be on your guard. The same notices are now going up alongside calls to annual novenas and the next meeting of the youth club in churches all over Ireland. The church at Monageer has its own entry in the documentary record of the child abuse scandals. An incident that happened here is recounted in the infamous Ferns Report.

In April 1988 ten girls told social workers of how they had been molested by the elderly parish priest on the altar while he was hearing their confessions. The priest sat on a chair while the children knelt on red cushions at his feet and the rest of the class, sitting in the pews, were told to keep their eyes closed because they were in a house of God. The priest would take a child's hands in his hands and pull them towards his half unzipped trousers. Then he would pull the child towards him and rub his face and mouth around their jaw as he questioned them. The children also described how he had put his hands under their skirts and fondled their legs 'to mid-thigh level only'.

The allegations themselves and the manner in which they were handled created divisions among parishioners at the time and I got the impression Father Cosgrave was reluctant to talk about it. The scandals hover over the Catholic Church in Ireland like some devastating family indiscretion, well known but unspoken. When I mention the policy statement in the porch to Father Cosgrave it is as if I have reminded him of something entirely ordinary, like drawing attention to the presence of a holy water font. 'Oh yes. That's what we have to do now,' he replies, before hurrying me to the car because he has to drive to Boolavogue to say another Mass at eleven. Today the quick turnaround is because the priest in the neighbouring parish is sick, but saying back-to-back Masses may soon become a way of life for Irish priests as the older generations die off and there are no new priests to replace them.

The church at Boolavogue has recently been refurbished; it is airier and lighter than the one we have left, with a stained-glass window at the back. It is also colder because Father Cosgrave doesn't understand the controls for the heating. The size of the congregation is remarkably similar to that at the last church: forty-one adults and a baby; ten men, none of them under thirty-five, and two teenagers with their mothers. Father Cosgrave repeats his sermon on how Mary's chastity is no longer her most winning attribute. People seem glad to be able to get away, except for a woman and her daughters, who gather around the mother of the baby at the back of the church to admire the child.

Father Cosgrave is stoical about the poor attendance at Mass. There is, he says, no sense of obligation any more. People who used to go regularly have given up and certainly anyone under fifty only comes occasionally. The practice of confession has declined even more dramatically. He doesn't seem to regret that, though; as he says, it had become a habit, with everybody rattling off the same sins. Ultimately, he says, the fear has gone out of religion.

His normal day begins with Mass at nine-thirty (there might be about twenty people there every day). After breakfast he attends to the letters and correspondence on his desk. Sometimes he might be given lunch by some local ladies at one of their houses. And then, in the afternoon, he drops in on people's houses or the school. As we drove past bungalows and slowed down to allow cars to pass on the narrow road I wondered what these people talked to their priest about; if they brought him their problems or asked him for advice. He seemed a little surprised by the question. He wasn't a social worker, he told me; he didn't seek out lame dogs and people didn't come to him looking for consolation.

Father Cosgrave has been a priest since 1965. His vocation, as he describes it, meant imbibing a feeling in his family that one of the children at least should become a priest. There was the bishop whose portrait hangs on the wall above his desk and an old tradition among respectable Irish farmers that with their eldest sons guaranteed to inherit the land their other children should look to the Church or the civil service or teaching for a living. Father Cosgrave had heard that after he was born his father had said, 'We'll put a collar on this fellow.' The certainty that the collar confers status and authority has dissolved in the last four decades. A priest used to be classed by the common people as one of their ruling elite, 'the big knobs' as people in rural Ireland call those who consider themselves superior. And even more than status the priest held a power that he could exercise with impunity. 'Fifty years ago if a lad saw the parish priest coming along the road he might jump over a ditch. A priest might give you a box in the mouth. And you would take it. Now you might get a box back.' The modern priest, according to Father Cosgrave, is a diminished figure providing the remnants of religion to his apathetic parishioners, respected if he does a reasonable job and puts on a good show. I took this to mean being there to receive a bride and groom at the altar, pour water on a baby's head at the baptismal font or stand in a cloud of incense mumbling prayers over a coffin. Anything more – any great vision of how religion could transform the world, any sense of mission – was out. Father Cosgrave is interested in new ideas – he's much taken by the notion of emotional intelligence – and the idea that the Church is in what he calls 'maintenance mode' clearly disappoints him.

I talked to Father Cosgrave about the impact of the decline in influence of religion in Ireland. I kept asking in different ways if he could tell me how a secular Ireland was worse off than the Ireland of the 1950s, when thousands went to Knock and people carried their banners around Lourdes in August. Despite all my questions, reformulated in various ways, I felt he wasn't able to clearly explain to me what good that kind of religion had done and what was lost by its disappearance. He often said he didn't know and I wasn't sure if this diffidence was some genuine perplexity or a disguised loss of faith on his part. In the end he said that all he could do was accept it; being a priest was the job he had chosen to do forty-three years ago. He couldn't do anything else; he had enough to do to keep going and not throw in the towel. He conceded that perhaps he should feel sad about it, but it was the way things were. It was like the Wexford hurling team, he said, suddenly arrested by a metaphor that would clarify everything. You would love to go to Croke Park to see Wexford win an All Ireland, but you know it is not going to happen.

In Enniscorthy the rain had stopped and the wintry blue sky was darkening. The Christmas lights were strung across the streets: Santa in a sleigh, a candle, a lantern, laughing snowmen. In the window of Delaney's newsagents they were selling a box of six Disney princess crackers and below it a picture of the Sacred Heart for €4.99. I walked a street that disappeared down a hill, the smell of turf smoke and vinegar in the air. I passed the Beriozka shop selling the finest foods from Eastern Europe. In a cafe, they were talking on the radio about how the Poles were going home in greater numbers. In Market Square, where a big Christmas tree had been raised in front of the council offices, two ten-year-old girls were sitting on a bench sucking Coke from cardboard cups with straws. Car engines puffed exhaust fumes into the air as the traffic backed up and people passed by going 'hiya' into their mobile phones. ∎

OUT OF GAS

As petrol becomes a 'distress purchase',
what happens to disused filling stations?

Craig Taylor

W hen a petrol station closes, the outgoing owner seals the petrol
lines, screeds the manholes, boards up the pumps and fills the
tanks with expanding foam. Not long after, the dandelions get their
way, pushing through the forecourt. Then come the knotweed and the
tubes of purple buddleia. The pigeons, free of human hassle, seek out
cracks in the canopy. Everything of value goes from the shop, although
the fridges and fire extinguishers may be left long enough to be stolen.
Sometimes a ridge of concrete is placed around the perimeter to keep
out caravans, yet dirty blankets and syringes offer evidence of those
who make it inside. Gradually an abandoned petrol station becomes a
destination for new forms of life: the fly-tippers, graffiti taggers, curious
photographers and landscape-waste dumpers.

Petrol stations were once fully staffed gateways to the open road.
Even if the architecture of British outfits couldn't match the opulence
of those in America, there were still attempts to advertise the romance
of travel and celebrate an abundance of oil. The Americans stuck
pumps inside fake Greek temples and flying saucers and in Los

Deserted petrol station, Down Thomas, Devon

Angeles, one station rested under a triangular canopy that jutted towards the tips of the palm trees. In Britain, Gulf designed a curved roof for its forecourts; elsewhere, there was a station housed in an art deco building in Plymouth and, in Cheshire, behind a stained-glass frontage, suggesting that the place was almost deserving of worship.

Filling stations were emblematic of the touring life, of transience and danger. The sexual betrayal in *The Postman Always Rings Twice* took place at one, though that particular affair seemed unique to North America's open roads. 'Could this tale of sex and murder ever happen in a petrol station on the outskirts of Stoke Poges?' asked Paul Barker in the *New Humanist* a few years ago. 'You must be joking. Garfield, Turner and her Greek husband would sit down for camomile tea and a chat.' Today, petrol stations are neither cosy nor audacious – they're little more than over-lit sheds, or mini-supermarkets with pumps attached. Petrol is no longer an idealized commodity administered by men in overalls who wipe windscreens and peer into engines, but rather a guilty necessity, requiring excuses and self-justification. With the knowledge that driving is terrible for the collective health of our planet goes any sense of pleasure and freedom. Those in the trade now call petrol a 'distress purchase' rather than a 'considered buy'. You only go when you're desperate – when the needle's low – and even then you might pass a few abandoned stations before you find a survivor.

There are now over 9,000 petrol stations in Britain, but in 2000 there were 13,107. The rate of site closures hovers at around 150 stations a year, though more than 500 stations closed only three years ago, according to the monitoring company Experian Catalist. Independent retailers mostly blame Esso who, in 1996, rolled out a scheme called Pricewatch in an effort to undercut competitors and halt the growing market share of supermarkets. The tactic was fought by the supermarkets, which used stations as loss-leaders: the costs of equipping and regulating a forecourt in the parking lot of a branch of Tesco, for example, was worthwhile for shops that turned over a million pounds a week. Caught between petrol giants and supermarkets, independent stations couldn't cover themselves, nor could they justify rebuilding, and when the economic reasons to pump petrol disappeared, so did the bright roadside signage for Elf, Fina, Mobil and Q8. Ten years ago, when property began to boom, abandoned sites in towns were sold to be turned into flats. The sites did not need to lie fallow. Planning permission could be granted as soon as the tanks left if the station's surroundings were not particularly dirty. Other stations in less desirable locations fell into disrepair and those that remained began to turn away from their chief product. Suddenly the number of Mars bars sold in the shop began to matter.

Luke Wilkinson has worked on petrol stations for over fifteen years and is now a technical director at SLR, an environmental consultancy that assesses contaminated sites. He has a special interest in petrol stations and carries various useful tools in the back of his Audi, as well as a supply of green gloves so he doesn't get his hands dirty prising open the squares of reinforced plastic that cover manholes on the forecourt. He studied geology and then, instead of going to work for an oil company, pursued a PhD focusing on renewable energy sources. He was attached to a project that involved heating water using the natural properties of granite in Cornwall, but the funding eventually disappeared. 'So I went to work for an oil company,' he says with a smile.

When he started his current job he was called on to help with due diligence in the buying and selling of petrol stations, but in the twenty-first century, he explained, 'It became all about decommissioning and checking safety. This is what we call a mature industry.' In his ten years with the company he's spent a lot of time on these flat, derelict sites at the side of major roads, plunging detection equipment deep beneath the tarmac to test for contamination in the soil and the water table. He showed me a cylinder of plastic attached to metres of green string. The groundwater inside carried the faint smell of petrol.

There are simple reasons for derelict sites. 'It's cheaper to just leave the pumps,' Wilkinson explained. We stood on the forecourt of a station in Cirencester where the pumps were boxed in with the same heavy plywood that covered the windows. The wind whistled past the abandoned Texaco signage. 'It's all still intact because there's no money to be made from selling old pumps and signs. Texaco is not particularly worried about leaving these remnants behind.' For Wilkinson, each forecourt offers clues to the history of petrol in Britain. Some sites contain more than a hundred years' worth of information – such as those where stations were built on quarries or old smithies, or at sites where the village petrol station had expanded. There are still mysteries on the forecourts. He walked past the plywood cladding and pointed out a marking on the tarmac. 'Down there is probably a five-hundred-gallon tank. It's small but it's still got paraffin in it,' he said. 'There were still seven hundred litres when we checked it. It's been there for maybe thirty years because no one buys paraffin any more. Things get forgotten. Things get lost.'

There is a site on the A40 near Oxford where the abandoned station has collapsed and trees have split the tarmac so that it looks now like nothing more than a scruffy lay-by. On the A38 near Derby another lies under a cover of rubble, dust and crushed brick. That, perhaps, is why such places appeal to photographers: American Jeff Brouws's work stresses the bleak lines of ambitious, disused American stations; Eric Tabuchi moves his camera closer to capture the look of rectangular canopies standing stark against the sky. Add to that thousands of online pictures from amateur photographers all over the world who are drawn to the rust and the piles of bricks – a post-apocalyptic vision easily within distance of a main road. Then there are photographers who see some of their own life in these damaged structures. A man named Frank Eye spent the winter of 2005–6 taking black-and-white photographs of 444 former filling stations. 'The bleak urban landscapes are a contrast with more optimistic times past,' reads the introduction on his website, 'and are an autobiographical reflection of the artist's own experience of being made redundant…'

The stations aren't just derelict on the surface. Beneath many of them is a 'plume of petrol', a slow spread of liquid seeping through the ground, getting darker as it leaches bitumen from the old tarmac. 'Historically, the tankers delivering petrol had flexible hoses,' Wilkinson said. 'Every time they unhooked the hose a little drip of fuel would leak out. A site that demands ten million litres of fuel would need three hundred deliveries a year. Every time the hose is used maybe 100ml gets spilled. Do that for thirty years and over time you can end up with contamination outside the tank and in the ground. In the worst case the plume travels fifty to one hundred metres.' He pointed at a white sign across the road to demonstrate the distance. Most sites pose no great hazard; only around ten per cent need represent a danger. The solution might take the form of vacuum extraction, where vapour is collected on a carbon filter. Sometimes the soil in question is excavated, treated and put back.

Soon the station where we stood in Cirencester will again become a working petrol station, albeit with a large Budgens grocery shop attached. It was not a welcoming structure on that windy day. 'It just looks really unhappy,' Wilkinson said as we got back in his car. Unhappy, perhaps, but resilient. 'It's not often you get a sense of a petrol station really returning to nature. It would just take too long. There's too much hard surfacing, too much infrastructure.' And so they sit, decaying slowly. The empty shells of Shells and, in our case, a Texaco receding in Wilkinson's rear-view mirror. ∎

MISSING

Eighteen years ago, toddler Ben Needham
disappeared on the Greek island of Kos.
How has his family coped?

Melanie McFadyean

When Madeleine McCann went missing, in May 2007, from the
bedroom of her parents' holiday villa in Portugal while they
had dinner nearby, it started one of the biggest international media
stories of recent years. The same photograph of Madeleine, a pretty
blonde three-year-old with a distinctive black mark in the iris of one
eye, was published day after day, as were pictures of her parents, Kate
McCann, a family GP, and Gerry McCann, a heart specialist, from
Leicester, always close together, with Kate McCann holding Cuddle
Cat, Madeleine's favourite toy.

Around the world people watched as they were flown from the
holiday resort of Praia da Luz, in the jet owned by billionaire retailer
Sir Philip Green, to meet Pope Benedict XVI in Rome; as wealthy
benefactors, Sir Richard Branson among them, donated time and
money to their cause. They spoke directly to Gordon Brown on the
phone. Diplomats supported them. Clarence Mitchell, a former
BBC journalist, left his job in the government's Central Office of
Information's media monitoring unit to run 'team McCann' and act

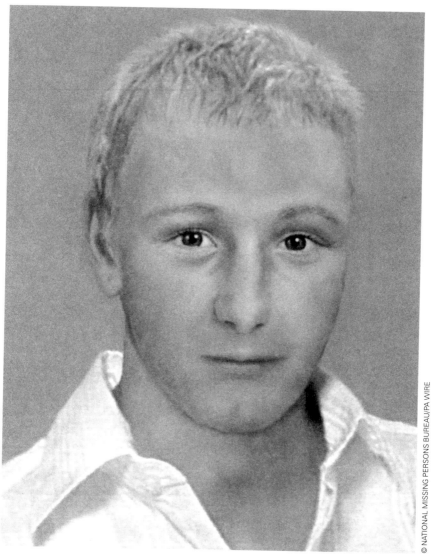

A digitally created image, released by the police in October 2007, showing how Ben Needham might look at the age of eighteen

as gatekeeper to the huge press onslaught. The children's author J. K. Rowling, the footballer Wayne Rooney and pop entrepreneur Simon Cowell contributed to the £2.5 million reward.

By September, the Portuguese police had named the McCanns as *arguidos*, suspects, in their daughter's disappearance. It wasn't until July 2008 that they were officially cleared. By this time they had sued Express Newspapers for stories falsely suggesting they were responsible for Madeleine's death and had disposed of her body. The McCanns received over half a million pounds in damages, which was paid into the 'Find Madeleine' fund. In January 2009, Gerry McCann flew back to Portugal to revive the attempts to find his daughter.

When Ben Needham disappeared from a farmhouse on the Greek island of Kos, in July 1991, while being looked after by his grandparents, the reaction had been very different. He was twenty-one months old, as blond and photogenic as Madeleine McCann, but this was before the days of the mobile phone, the Internet, the instant transmission of news; before Princess Diana's death legitimized the collective outpouring of public emotion that now accompanies so many catastrophes. And Kerry Needham and Simon Ward, an unmarried couple from a Sheffield housing estate, didn't have the same appeal as the professional, middle-class McCanns.

I first met the Needhams in September 1993. By then, their story was only sporadically in the news. I had been in Crete that summer with my two-year-old son. Haunted by Ben Needham's story, I never let him out of my sight. One afternoon, in a village in the hills, I was chatting to two old women outside a cafe when a child playing nearby caught my eye. He had tawny blond hair, pale eyes and a T-shirt with 'Kos' written on it. He didn't look Greek. One of the old women said he came from a villa a few yards away, but nobody knew the people who lived there.

I took a photograph of the boy and sent it to the Needhams via South Yorkshire Police. It wasn't Ben. In September, I went to see the Needhams in their council house in Sheffield to interview them for the

Guardian. They were easy to find; journalists could ring them directly and go and see them. Over the years they have hoped publicity will keep Ben in the public's thoughts.

In 1993, Kerry Needham, Ben's mother, was twenty-one. She was thin, quiet and withdrawn. Her father, Eddie, did the talking. Her mother, Christine, kept out of the way; she let Eddie deal with the press. Since then I have stayed in touch with the Needhams. In 1996 I worked on a documentary about Ben Needham's disappearance for Channel 4, and I have written about them periodically.

Kerry Needham's was never a household name. In some ways this was a good thing – she didn't suffer the constant pressure of media scrutiny that Gerry and Kate McCann underwent – but it had its downside: the story slipped out of sight and to most people she and Ben were almost forgotten. But when Madeleine McCann disappeared, the press remembered Kerry and she was bombarded with calls. The attention brought a sudden rush of emotions.

'I was devastated for the McCanns,' she told me last July, 'but it wiped me out to the point where I needed tablets again. One day I did twenty-seven interviews. Watching them on television took me back – living that day again. And it made me bitter and angry because the official help that they got was unbelievable: the British ambassador gave a statement at a press conference, British police officers flying over, a visit with the Pope, phone calls from Gordon Brown…'

Gordon Brown was reported to have intervened when the McCanns were frustrated by lack of progress in the investigation. Encouraged by this, Kerry wrote to Gordon Brown. It took him three months to respond and his reply, when it came, gave her no hope. 'He told me what the British authorities had done in all these years, but nothing about what could be done. I know what's been done and it's not enough. He wrote that the Greek authorities would reopen the case if there was a promising new line of enquiry.' In her letter Kerry told him that a white car had been seen in the area the day Ben disappeared, and the police knew who owned it, but that there has been no conclusive investigation into it. She was surprised Brown didn't pick up on this.

She also wrote to her local MP, David Blunkett, in November, clearly spelling out the uninvestigated lead. He responded swiftly and positively, saying he would approach the Home and Foreign secretaries to contact Interpol and pressurize the Greek authorities to look at this 'additional potential lead'. Kerry then had a letter from the Home Secretary, Jacqui Smith, in which she said she had passed the information on to the chief constable of South Yorkshire Police.

'I've gone round the houses and been sent back to South Yorkshire Police. It still doesn't give me the answer I want, but I'll continue to push for Ben. They're still not telling me if this can be investigated or if Ben's case can be reinvestigated from the start.'

In January 2008 Kerry was contacted by a television director, who was making a documentary about the McCanns. As Kerry remembers it, she was asked if she would like to meet Kate McCann, and she said she would, as long as there were no cameras and no reporters and they could meet as one bereft mother with another. But the meeting never took place. When I spoke to Clarence Mitchell in November 2008, he said that the film director hadn't asked Kerry if she wanted to meet Kate McCann, but whether she would appear in the documentary as the mother of a lost child. 'Kate finds the idea of meeting a parent in that position quite daunting,' he told me then. '[Kerry] has been living with it for eighteen years and the idea of facing it as long and stoically as Kerry has is a bit daunting. It's not that she doesn't want to meet her, she's sure she's a lovely person and maybe one day she will feel like it. But she doesn't want to face a lifetime without finding Madeleine.'

So when a letter arrived out of the blue on January 24 this year from Kate McCann, Kerry was amazed. 'I thought it was sweet of her. I didn't think she would ever get in contact with me. I was really moved, it's a really heartfelt letter. She'd wanted to be in touch with me but had been scared of having to admit that Madeleine's disappearance might end up like Ben's. Nobody wants to think that a child could be missing for years and years. If the boot had been on the other foot I wouldn't have wanted to get in touch with somebody whose child had been missing for all these years because it would give you no hope. You'd think, is that me in eighteen years?'

As banal as it seems, this is the one question you have to ask: how have Kerry and her family endured the years without Ben? 'We've survived,' Kerry said. 'We've all found a way. I don't know what way it is – but a way of coping with it. We've found the strength to live and cope and we'll never get over it even though we deal with it. But we can never understand it.'

This is the story of how these eighteen years have been for each of the family since Ben disappeared.

There is never a day, Kerry says, that Ben isn't in her thoughts. If she believed he were dead it might be easier. There would be a focus for that grief, a conclusion. But her family is still convinced that Ben was snatched, and Kerry's instincts tell her that her son is alive and out there, somewhere.

Ben, who in his absence is the epicentre of his family, would now be nineteen. In 2003 the Metropolitan Police released a digitally enhanced photograph of how he might look at twelve: a smiling butter-blond boy who didn't resemble anyone in his family. A second digital photograph, in which he slightly resembles Kerry's brother Stephen, was made in 2007, when he would have been eighteen. It has the unsettling qualities of both a passport photo and a criminal photofit.

Ben was born in October 1989 when Kerry was seventeen. She had met his father, Simon Ward, when she was fifteen and still at school. The Needhams come from South Yorkshire: Eddie Needham, a builder by trade, is from Chapeltown, near Sheffield, and his wife, Christine, from Thorpe Hesley, a mining village outside Rotherham. They met as teenagers and married soon afterwards. In the early 1980s, then in their mid-thirties, they moved to Chapel St Leonards, near Skegness, on the Lincolnshire coast. At first they lived on the caravan site where in the past they had spent summer holidays: Eddie worked on a building site and collected scrap metal; Christine worked in a fish-and-chip shop then rented a cafe, which she ran. Later she worked as a supervisor in a hardware store. They did well and eventually bought a house.

In the summer of 1990, Christine's sister treated the family to their first foreign holiday on the Greek island of Kos. Christine fell in love with the island and with life in the sun. At the end of that year the Needhams sold everything they had, bought an old Land-Rover and a caravan, and set off to live on Kos. Their two sons, Danny, then eleven, and Stephen, seventeen, went with them. Kerry stayed behind in Sheffield, where she had moved with Simon, missing her family and hating their damp and dingy flat. Simon worked away from home and she was often alone. Eventually, in April 1991, she and Ben, who was eighteen months old, went out to join them. She had never even been to London, let alone on a plane or to a foreign country.

Once on Kos, Kerry blossomed. She lived in a bedsit, shared the care of Ben with her mother and found work at a hotel serving snacks around the pool. She had felt justified in leaving Simon behind. Kerry told me that Simon left when she was five months pregnant. 'I had no money, living on bread and jam, no life whatsoever,' she'd told me. He didn't come back until Ben was born.

On Kos, Christine, who had been working in the same hotel as Kerry serving drinks and snacks, gave up her job to take care of Ben. Kerry upgraded from the bedsit to a small holiday flat and Ben stayed either with her or with the rest of the family in the caravan, which was parked in an olive grove in an area called Paradisi, near the beach, about ten minutes' walk from Kos town.

Eddie and Stephen had found work renovating a small farmhouse a couple of miles outside the town in a hilly area known as Herakles. The owner had told them that if they did it up, the Needhams could live in the house rent-free, in return for looking after it when he was away.

On July 24, Christine, Eddie, Danny, Stephen and the owner of the house, Michaelis Kypreos, were inside the farmhouse eating lunch and sheltering from the heat. Ben was playing on the terrace just outside the door. He was running in and out, pouring water over his head and messing about with a stick he'd been trailing in some ashes. They could see through the open door on to the terrace where Ben was playing. There was a tree on which they'd hung Ben's wet shorts.

At about two-thirty, Stephen left on his moped to go for a swim, a beer and a shower at Kerry's flat. Ben wanted to go with him; he'd been on the bike before, and now he wanted to go with his uncle.

A few minutes after Stephen left, Christine registered that Ben had gone quiet and went outside. He was nowhere to be seen. She, Eddie, Danny and Michaelis Kypreos searched up and down the lane, in the field at the side of the house, in a nearby orange grove, calling for him, looking anywhere he could conceivably be. When they couldn't find him, they assumed he must have gone with Stephen; it was the only logical explanation. They thought Stephen must have taken Ben for a ride and would bring him back.

About an hour later, thinking Stephen had gone to the caravan instead of coming back to the farmhouse, or had gone to Kerry's flat, Christine walked back to Paradisi, while Eddie, Danny and Kypreos stayed working on the roof.

In the early evening Eddie went to the caravan expecting to find Ben with Christine. He wasn't, so Eddie went to Kerry's flat, thinking he would be there. Stephen was there, but without Ben. Eddie raced back to the caravan to tell Christine and then went back to Herakles in the Land-Rover. Stephen took Christine to the police on his bike and then joined his father. It was several hours since Ben had vanished by the time the police took Christine to the hotel to tell Kerry what had happened. Kerry had finished her shift and was sitting by the swimming pool when her mother arrived, sobbing, to tell her Ben had disappeared.

The police took them both to Herakles to join Eddie and the boys. They searched, going to places that Ben could never have got to, covering some fifteen acres, through olive groves and pomegranate orchards, riverbeds and long grass.

The next day Kos police began their investigation and their first questions were directed at the Needhams. They were immediately hostile to Kerry. 'They banged their hands on the table,' she told me.

'They shouted, "Where is boy? How can you lose baby? Why do you go to work? You must not love your child."'

She had been unaware of the image local people had of her. They had always seemed friendly, but after Ben disappeared, island gossip found its way back to her – she was an unfit mother, a slut. Why wasn't she married? Why did she work and not look after her child? Her family lived like gypsies in a caravan. Kerry didn't love Ben, she'd given him away, she'd sold him...

The sightings started within twenty-four hours. The first was a child seen buying sweets at the airport, but news of it took three days to get to the Needhams. Over the next few years there were to be hundreds of reports of small blond children in situations perceived as being suspicious.

It took a few days for the news of Ben's disappearance to filter through to the UK press. The first to knock at the caravan door was a reporter from the *Sun*. In the next few weeks reporters came from other national newspapers, both tabloid and broadsheet, and from TV news stations; but there was none of the frenzied coverage that engulfed the McCanns.

The family stayed on Kos for two months after Ben disappeared. Then Eddie rang the British Embassy in Athens to ask if they could be repatriated. There had been no progress with the investigation and the strain on them was unbearable. Eddie said his family was on the verge of breakdown, they had to get home. He was told that they would have to be means-tested and it might be a month before that was complete. And so, desperate to get back to England, they sold everything they had and arrived home at the end of September, broke.

They went back to Yorkshire, and at first they were split up, living with various relatives in Sheffield, before being housed by the council.

The second time I met Kerry was in 1996. I was working on a Channel 4 documentary about Ben. The silent, passive girl who had sat in the lee of her father's body three years before had become spiky and edgy. By this time, she had a daughter, Leighanna. She and

Simon Ward had drifted back together and Kerry had got pregnant. Leighanna was born in February 1994; not long after, Simon went to prison for five years, charged with robbery.

It was a long time before Kerry had been able to articulate what those early months had been like after Ben went missing. She and Simon were living together again. 'I used to get up in the middle of the night and it was like I was hallucinating that Ben was actually there. We'd decorated a bedroom for him and I used to go in there and pretend to rock him to sleep because I thought I could hear him crying. I had a psychiatric nurse who was wonderful, and she said that having the bedroom there was making it worse. Obviously I was dreaming that I could hear him crying and I was just automatically, as a mum, getting up in the middle of the night and going to rock the baby.'

The only release came with sleep. She took pills. If woken by a dream, she'd take some more. She made four suicide attempts. She overdosed on antidepressants and attempted to cut her wrists, but says she knows she didn't really want to die. It was more that edging around death brought temporary relief from the pain.

It had been people close to her – the community psychiatric nurse, her maternal grandmother – who suggested she have another baby. 'They said those maternal instincts that woke me in the middle of the night would be of use if I had another baby.'

She looked at photographs of her son and at snapshots tourists had taken of children they thought might be Ben, but never were. She wrote him letters. A few times she roused herself and went with television crews or journalists following up sightings of Ben. In 1992, for example, she went on a trip to Izmir, in Turkey. The photo of the child had been very like Ben, but the child was a girl. Kerry broke down. The child's mother passed her daughter to her, letting Kerry hold her.

There were hundreds of sightings, none of them Ben: BLOND BOY BEGGING ON ATHENS UNDERGROUND. BLOND BOY CLEANING CAR WINDOWS IN ATHENS WATCHED BY DARK-SKINNED WELL-DRESSED MAN. The expectation and disappointment of these trips threatened

Kerry's sanity. Eddie encouraged her to stay out of it and let him rove the world looking for Ben instead.

The arrival of a new baby, physically similar to the one who was lost, had brought Kerry out of her paralysis, but Leighanna couldn't replace Ben and Kerry found it hard to be her mother. She went through the motions of motherhood but it brought her no joy. 'I couldn't be anyone,' she says, 'only Ben Needham's mum. But I couldn't be his mum because he wasn't there. I couldn't cope with being me, I couldn't be a real person. I couldn't cope with anything. It was tough on Leighanna and tough on me. I plodded on but it was a really awful time.'

By 1996, Leighanna was living with Eddie and Christine. They were looking after their granddaughter but Kerry felt they were furious with her. 'We have always been very close,' said Christine, 'the family has been entwined, the bonds are so strong, and we've cried and cried and hugged and hugged and been almost too close or hated each other.' They were afraid it would appear as if she had abandoned her child and public perceptions of Ben's case would suffer as a consequence. They were horrified when a story appeared in the *Sheffield Star*: KERRY GIVES UP HER DAUGHTER. Two days later, there was another in the *Sunday Express*: 'I DON'T WANT MY SON BACK', SAYS MOTHER AS SHE SHUNS NEW BABY. Kerry had spoken unguardedly to reporters. It was true that she couldn't cope with her new baby, but not that she didn't want Ben back.

For the past few months she had submerged herself in the Sheffield club scene and was working in a club bar. Her parents thought she was selfish and irresponsible. For Kerry it was an escape. But even there she was recognized: 'I was in the toilets at the club and this woman was looking at me, "You're Ben Needham's mum... I wouldn't be out if it had happened to me." I said, "What do you know?" I pinned her up against the toilet door.'

At that time, she said, people found her cold and hard because she didn't cry when asked about Ben. Her grief had given way to anger: she was angry that he had been taken, angry because not enough was being done at an official level, angry that her life had been destroyed when Ben went missing.

In the spring of 1997, when Leighanna was nearly three, Simon Ward's father died. Although she no longer felt close to Simon (by the time he came out of prison, their relationship was over), Kerry suddenly felt a pang about her own father, her family, her daughter. 'It made me realize life is short and I wanted to be with them.' She went to her parents' house, frightened she might not be welcome. As she walked in Leighanna glanced up from a book she was looking at and greeted her mother as though no time had passed. Kerry sat reading to her. Eddie, Kerry says, 'huffed and puffed for a bit'. She had to prove that she was capable of having Leighanna back.

Kerry was lucky: her daughter came home willingly and they settled down. Even then, Kerry's life was not without drama. A three-year relationship ended badly, and another with a nightclub manager ended when he was stabbed to death in a street brawl. She had a brief holiday romance in Dominica with a man who conned her out of £500. I'd heard bits of Kerry's story from Christine and Eddie in the years since I'd seen her, but I didn't know how she would be when I went to visit her in Sheffield in June last year.

Kerry has always been slight; her face is narrow and delicate and she moves quickly and neatly. In her living room, my eye was drawn to two things: on the centre of the mantelpiece, the last picture of Ben taken before he vanished, and, to the right, a large birdcage and a parrot. It screeched, 'Shut up! Fucking hell Ziggy!' Kerry laughed. Ziggy the parrot came with Craig Grist, a builder, the man she married in 2006.

I asked Kerry how she feels now when she is interviewed. She lit a cigarette. She said she hates being asked what she would say to Ben if she found him now. But she responds openly to most enquiries because every time a bit of her gets out there it might reach Ben, and it reminds people about him. Kerry has taken the lead in the search for Ben, although there are few sightings now.

Her efforts to have Ben's case reopened mean that she is anxious that all uninvestigated leads are followed up. One of them involves a trip to Kos in July 2000 when she went with her father, Stephen and Leighanna to collect Ben's case file, which they had been told they could have. While they were there, Eddie asked the policeman who had been in charge of the case about the white car seen in the lane in Herakles at around two-thirty on the afternoon Ben vanished. The policeman told Eddie who it belonged to. To the Needhams' amazement, it was someone they knew, but this was the first they had heard of it. 'There may be a perfectly good explanation,' said Kerry, but she'd like to know it has been properly investigated and feels it hasn't been. There are other unresolved leads, and Kerry's priority is for the authorities to investigate them.

In the years since Ben went missing, she has often felt on the edge of sanity.

'I often ask myself, am I normal?' she said. 'It's like looking in on other people's lives and I think sometimes, am I insane or if I'm not insane, why am I not? Some people don't get over one trauma in their life, be it a death or an affair or a cot death or an abortion. So why have I made it, if I have made it, after everything?' She tapped her head. 'What has it done to me up here?'

In the years after Ben's disappearance, Eddie and Christine Needham restarted their lives. They had a friend who ran the local tip in Sheffield and in the late 1990s they started looking there for things to sell at car boot sales. They graduated to the antiques fair at Swinderby in Yorkshire and from the local tip to bigger tips. For three years, until they left England again in 2004, they ran three tips. To their surprise they made enough money to buy a house in Cyprus and return to Christine's dream of a life in the sun.

They had been on a holiday to Turkish Cyprus. Once again they uprooted themselves. They bought a villa overlooking the sea on the side of a hill in the village of Alsancak on the north coast. They renovated the house and Christine made a garden. In June 2008, I flew to Cyprus to meet her. When I arrived I rang her and to my surprise she asked me to meet her several hours' drive away in Dipkarpaz, in the north-east of the island. She had left Eddie. He didn't know where she was and she was going to keep it that way: she was going to stay there, read books and grow vegetables.

I met her in a beach cafe. She looked tanned and her hair was bleached blonde. She was wearing white-framed sunglasses, smoking a cigarette and gazing out to sea.

I remembered being with Christine in Greece, in 1996, during the making of the Channel 4 film, and the way she had described what it was like when they first moved to Kos. 'It was free, like being on a permanent high,' she said. 'Sunny, peaceful, there was only the crickets. It was like living in a free world.

'Most people wouldn't say, "Let's just go and live in Greece". So we'd achieved something. We had money in the bank, not a lot, but we lived simply and had everything we needed…sea and olive trees and lemons growing on trees in the streets, like another world, a dream. And then Ben disappeared.'

It was Christine who had taken Ben to the farmhouse that day, while Kerry was at work. In Cyprus she described again what happened; how they'd been sitting inside, eating lunch, and Ben was playing, in and out, and then after Stephen left she couldn't hear him. 'I'm thinking – he's quiet. It's an instinct, you just know the quiet bit means trouble. God knows I never thought it would be that much trouble.'

She told me how they had assumed Stephen had given Ben a ride on his moped. 'He was mad for that bike,' she said. 'We've got pictures of him on it. We were waiting for the bike ride to finish, then ten minutes turned into half an hour and then you're thinking, "He's a long time".' About an hour later she'd said, 'It looks like Steve's not coming back. I'll get off now, get the tea on.'

It didn't occur to her that someone could have taken Ben. But if someone had, wouldn't he have screamed? 'It depends. If they'd got sweets, that would shut him up straight away. You trust people at that age if they're kind; they hold you by the hand and take you. Like Jamie

Bulger [the toddler from Merseyside who was abducted and killed in 1993]. He didn't kick up a fuss. There's just no answer.'

The eight weeks they stayed on Kos after Ben disappeared were a blur, she said. 'I don't know how we kept alive, but in the first weeks you believe that the next day there'll be news, you're still hopeful and you're on automatic, survival kicks in.' She said they wandered round aimlessly, searching, or sat together going over every detail again and again, 'messing our brains up'. Kerry said her mother looked as if she was dying. 'There's a picture of us like skeletons,' Christine said. 'I can't remember feeding my family. I never cooked a meal. How cruel I was then – nobody fed Danny.

'You're on the edge of your balance in your mind,' she continued. 'You're not the same person ever again. You cope with everyday things but something at some point will turn you over the edge and then you think you're completely insane. I didn't think about killing myself because I thought that would put more grief on my family. I couldn't do that to them, it would have been the most selfish thing in the world to do.'

Her instinct has been to consolidate what there is left, to hold it together. In the first months at home she hankered after the ordinary. The sound of the Hoover and the washing machine soothed her. Eddie was enraged by the domesticity that kept Christine sane. He was obsessed with finding Ben, never off the phone, unable to talk about anything else. His voice, she said, was like a drill in her head.

'One Christmas, I burned all his clothes. Eddie's not as bad-tempered as me but I'd be angry and I'd leave, sometimes for an hour, sometimes for three weeks.

'All of a sudden life changes,' she said. 'We had a normal life, then Ben is lost and we are in another world, a world where people come out of the shadows at you and others talk of guns. All this madness. You can't believe it's happened because if you did you'd probably go insane. Sometimes I bury my head in the sand so I don't feel it. Perhaps that's how I deal with it, so it isn't as painful. It's like half-pretending isn't it?'

'We lost our grandson through our stupidity,' she said some years ago. 'Through not acting quickly, presuming he was all right, we've been irresponsible. It's our fault.' Now she says her guilt came from a 'failure to be on alert'.

'It felt so safe, there was no traffic, no people. I have brought up my family haphazardly, maybe, but they are all safe, and then I get this one job to look after Ben one day and I don't do it properly. I relaxed. There seemed to be no danger. I wasn't vigilant.

'I've said to Kerry, "Why didn't you shout at me?" And she said, "Because I never blamed you." I thought I ought to feel guilty, because if somebody had lost my child, I would be at them. But my feeling isn't guilt, it's more a – what if? What if I'd done this differently? What if I hadn't gone there that day?'

One theory about Ben's disappearance is that he had somehow fallen into the hands of gypsies. In October 1996, Christine and Eddie had appeared on a live Greek TV phone-in show about missing people. A prisoner in jail in Larissa, in central Greece, called in saying he had seen Ben in March 1992 with a gypsy family in the town of Veria in northern Greece. Several other people called in independently, also locating Ben in Veria. It seemed the closest the Needhams had come to any real link to Ben.

In February 1997, I had gone to Veria with Christine to talk to some of the callers to the show. Most of them were scared, and didn't want to be identified. One woman said she and her husband had seen a striking blond child they thought was Ben in September 1996. She had overheard a conversation between the head of the gypsy family and another man. The gypsy had said, 'The kid is here. If they want to take him let them have him.' She hadn't gone to the police because she was afraid.

We also went to see a taxi driver who we had spoken to the year before. He'd told us then he was sure that Ben had been in his taxi in January 1994, with a female member of the gypsy family and some other children. When he had asked who the boy was, another child had told him it was Ben or Benzi, and the woman had threatened to smack him. When we saw the taxi driver again, he had been interviewed by the police and changed his mind.

We went to see the police. We were ushered into a room where a group of men were smoking and playing cards. One of them got up to speak to us. He said the prisoner was a 'mythomaniac' whose story couldn't be taken seriously.

In Athens Christine met a senior official from the Ministry of Public Order. He told us the gypsy was a criminal, a drug dealer and a car thief and that the prisoner was a liar. Nothing more came of the prisoner's story. It was all disturbing, dispiriting and futile.

At the end of the day I spent with Christine in Cyprus in June last year, as the sun went down, she said, 'We all cracked up in our own ways. And we've all tried to be someone else for a little while. But you take on this mother role, holding everybody up, especially Kerry, she was so delicate. I used to jolly them along. I didn't want my family to die. I thought everybody would commit suicide. Everybody thinks that I deal with it better than anybody else, but that is because I know they won't cope if I drop. If I go under, my family will die, I know they will, even now, they will.'

Last year, on the same trip to Cyprus, I went to visit Eddie. I found him sunk into the corner of a sofa in the living room of their villa in front of a large flat-screen TV with the sound turned off.

For years his whole being was concentrated on his crusade, as he called it, to find Ben. The night Ben went missing, Eddie and Stephen had driven to the port on Kos at three a.m. There was a line of trucks and cars waiting to board the ferry. Eddie and Stephen peered into the windows. They couldn't believe there were no police checking the vehicles. The policeman who had said he would join them there never turned up.

When they searched the fields around the farmhouse, they heard noises in the dark, like a baby, but never a baby, perhaps lambs or goats. As soon as it was light, Eddie searched sheds and outhouses. He went through bins, pulling out plastic sacks, dreading what he might find.

During the police interrogations he banged his fists on the table, enraged by the suggestion that 'our Kerry was a slut'. He spent three days next to a digger as it excavated the rubble of a demolished house on the lane in Herakles, bracing himself for the possibility that it would disgorge his grandson's body.

The police told him they thought Ben was alive: if there is a dead body, certain birds flock to it, they said, but no such birds had been seen. A stranger in a taverna told him to get a gun and go to the back-alley bars in Athens. That was where the answer lay. That was where children were bought and sold for illegal adoption or organ transplants. The police told him that gypsies sell babies and that little blond boys fetch the highest prices.

In those first days and nights Eddie said he heard Ben's voice in his head, urging him on, telling him he was nearly there, to go on trying to find him. He remembers collapsing on the road outside the hotel where Kerry worked, weeping. When he walked through a gypsy camp with posters in Greek publicizing Ben's disappearance, a woman thrust her pregnant daughter at him, offering her unborn baby for sale.

Eddie feels that his family was ignored by British officials. It still makes him angry. No British representative came to Kos in those first weeks after Ben vanished. Eddie says that when he pushed coins into a phone box to call the embassy in Athens, he was told that since none of his family was in jail they didn't need a lawyer, and since nobody was alone, and there were people around who spoke English, they didn't need an interpreter.

Back in England, Eddie kept up the search, losing count of the times he went to Greece, following sightings, sometimes with television crews and journalists, sometimes with Christine, occasionally with Kerry, often on his own. He did it on a shoestring, dependent on the press paying expenses or on scraping up a fare by standing outside rock concerts with buckets or selling stuff at car boot sales. He slept on beaches, or in cheap hotel rooms. He only spoke a few words of Greek and they were mostly to do with building. There were moments when, from a distance, the blond child they were going to see would look so like Ben they'd think they had found him.

At home, Eddie brooded, watched TV and waited by the phone. Unable to work, he signed on the dole. He found himself subject to fits of anger that he had never experienced before. He would listen to anyone, be cynical sometimes, surly on occasion, but always listening, even to the dowsers, clairvoyants and seventh sons of seventh sons who said Ben was in Florida, California, a Scandinavian country, 'taken by a man in a leather jacket with an Alsatian dog and he didn't go easily'.

Only a few weeks before my visit to Cyprus, the Sheffield police in charge of Ben's case in the UK had been told of a sighting of a young man in the Greek part of Cyprus, thought by a tourist to resemble how Ben might look now. Eddie had been to meet him. 'I wish it'd been my grandson, because he was a gentleman and I would have been very proud of him,' he said, 'but he was Romanian. Hugged him, kissed him, checked the birthmark on his neck just to make sure, that's how close it was. He didn't have the birthmark.'

Eddie seemed to me to be in that state of stupefied sobriety that comes after days and nights alone with the bottle. 'I'm just an ignorant person,' he said. 'I haven't got the intelligence to put the past behind me. Can you understand that?' I said I didn't think it was a matter of intelligence. 'Christine understands,' he said. 'She's got the brains, she can work it out and she knows it's too late, that I'm so thick and stupid I just carry on bulldozing through everything. The thought of Ben is there constantly. When I don't think about it I feel terrible, I feel guilty for not thinking about it.'

When I left he was with his younger son, Danny, who lives with them in Cyprus. A few days later, I went back to see him. He was sober and unexpectedly sanguine about Christine's continuing absence and her insistence that she would never return. Their thirty-nine years of marriage have been punctuated by Christine's intermittent departures, usually sparked by Eddie's occasional drinking. Christine had always returned within a week or two. Later, after Eddie had gone out shopping, Danny got a call to say that his father had collapsed in the street and been taken by ambulance to Kyrenia, forty-five minutes away. He was on a drip and about to be given a brain scan.

I went with Danny to the hospital. He told me that his father had been advised to give up smoking, and that if he didn't, he was going to be in trouble.

'They said I'd got type-two diabetes,' Eddie reported on the way back, strapped like a sparrow into the front seat. 'Got to reduce my sugar intake. Can't smoke in your car can I? Dying for a fag.'

We sat on the terrace drinking coffee. I asked him, though it was a trite question, whether he felt as if he'd ever got over the loss of Ben.

'How can you get over it?' he replied. 'How can I get over it? It's my fault. I should have looked after him. He was there one minute and the next minute he's gone, how can you explain that? I can't.'

Christine had telephoned him. 'I said to her, you come back here and live in the house because you love this house and the garden so much. You come back and I'll leave and she sent me a text saying, "It's not the house I love it's you."'

I asked how much he thought the volatility with Christine, the benders, have to do with losing Ben. He thought about it for a moment and then said, 'Everything. Nothing.'

There were three suits hanging from the spiral staircase that led to the first floor of the Needhams' Cyprus villa: a gold suit and two white ones, one with silver buttons down the outsides of the legs, the other with ruffles down the front. These were the costumes Danny Needham wore several nights a week when he went to work as Elvis, more tribute singer than impersonator.

When I'd first met Danny in 1993, he was thirteen. I'd talked to him as he walked his cat on the wasteland near their house with Christine picking her way after us. The next time I saw him he was sixteen and thinking about A levels. He'd passed them and been accepted at university to study film and television.

'I chose the university of life instead,' he told me when I saw him again in Cyprus. In 2000, he'd gone on holiday to Benidorm. He came back and said to his brother: 'Steve, do you want to be a millionaire?'

There were a million tourists in Benidorm, he told him, and there wasn't an ice-cream van in sight. So they bought an old Bedford minibus and painted it pink and blue. They bought sliding-top freezers and with some difficulty crossed Europe as they'd done with their parents a decade earlier. They kept the ice cream cold at night by plugging the freezer into the mains in their flat via a cable. There was a two-hour window when it could be unplugged and the ice cream would still be frozen and they could sell it. The police were just showing an interest when they were warned off by the local mafia and the dream ended.

Stephen came back to England, but Danny stayed in Benidorm. He took a job managing a bar, and before long he met another bar manager, a young Colombian, who played the guitar. Danny wrote poems and they started trying to write songs together. After hours they'd get on stage and sing. 'We were absolutely terrible,' he said, 'but we enjoyed it and we were learning from mucking about.'

After a few months he decided to try karaoke. 'I've loved Elvis since I was five, so I sang Elvis.' Soon he was singing several nights a week.

'One night a little old lady came up to me – I'd sung this song called "Don't" and she said, "I've been coming to Benidorm for twenty-two years. Me and my husband are both big Elvis fans. We've seen Elvis impersonators over the years and I've never heard anybody sing like that."'

This galvanized Danny. He returned to the UK and set about making a career in music. He bought backing tracks, a guitar, amps, mixers and microphones and practised every night. By day he worked at his father's tip. The outfit he'd bought at an Elvis shop in Nottingham – black leather trousers, black cowboy boots, a couple of red scarves, a gold rock 'n' roll-style jacket and a shiny black shirt – hung in the wardrobe. Nobody knew what he was doing. It took him about two years to teach himself to sing.

When his parents bought the house in Cyprus, Danny said he wanted to go with them. 'I told them I was going to do an Elvis show. My dad laughed his head off. He goes, "You can't sing." I said, "I know that, but I've been practising."' His parents were amazed when he came second in a pub karaoke competition in Lincoln and won £400. In Cyprus he was soon invited to sing at a big karaoke bar and then offered the Elvis gig five nights a week. Four years on, he'd learned about 250 Elvis songs and made it big along the expat coastal strip of northern Cyprus.

He says his memory of the day Ben vanished is like 'still frames' in his head.

'I remember being at the farmhouse, eating out of the sun. I can't remember Steve leaving. Then I remember Mum getting up and saying, "Where's Ben? He's gone quiet." I was at the age where Mum and Dad know best so I wasn't panicking. After an hour of looking we assumed that Steve had taken him. We sat around. Dad finished off, packed his tools. We went to Kerry's. Dad said, "Where's Ben?" Then panic. We drove to my mum and then to Herakles. It was dusk and getting darker. We were driving up the roads in the dark with the main beam on, to fences, up to gates, and we were climbing over them and we did this for hours.'

Though he was only eleven at the time, when he talks about Ben's disappearance, he refers to 'the biggest mistake we made', including himself in the frame. He says it was a mistake not to go right to the bottom of the lane, to assume that Ben couldn't have got that far. They might have seen a car, or someone running – something that might have led to Ben.

He described his feelings of grief. 'It's a big abyss of sadness that's in there. As long as you're occupied and stuff is going on... Then you just stop dead, and I can feel this thing... I think it's because of seeing my family hurt. Because I was the youngest one, I've just always been in the background and watched everybody else, seeing the pain that they've been through. You understand that as an adult. But I was just a kid. It was hard to understand exactly the thing that's happened. It's like a way that I feel in my stomach, butterflies, and I can fill up, I can feel it now, you can just fill up.

'My mum always says, "Why don't you talk about it? Talk to me about it." But I am actually fine. I've got no problems with the way I feel. You think *that was the saddest thing ever that could happen to me*, so everything else is a bonus. I laugh and smile every day, and a lot of people must think, how can we laugh and joke and have a good time and it's like, well, you've got to balance that sadness.'

In the evening I went to see him perform under arc lights strung between eucalyptus trees on the terrace of a big hotel. He was wearing the gold suit, and his shoes were freshly sprayed gold. He was framed by two life-sized photos of Elvis, with the Turkish flag on either side, and green baize underfoot. As he crooned into the microphone, his eyes closed, a small band of fans aged between two and eighty looked on, misty-eyed, or danced cheek to cheek while two toddlers with dummies in their mouths wobbled around.

He didn't see his father as he slipped into the back of the bar to watch him. Danny was singing his favourite Elvis song, 'The Impossible Dream'. As Danny came to the end of the song, Eddie made his way to the stage and put his arms around Danny, who led his father over to some of their friends sitting nearby.

Christine went back to Eddie a week after I saw them in June 2008.

D anny's older brother, Stephen Needham, lives in the Lincolnshire farm workers' cottage that was his parents' home until they moved to Cyprus. For most of his adult life he has worked on farms, on building sites, or for his father, helping to collect scrap metal. When I visited him last year, he was on disability benefit. He was born with Perthes' disease, a condition that causes the hip joints to crumble, and at seven he'd had a hip reconstruction. In the last few years it has started to cause him trouble and will need to be operated on again. 'So I'm on the scrap heap,' he said, ruefully, 'but I like pottering and gardening and decorating and drawing.'

Stephen looks a lot like Kerry. He has the same blond hair, the same narrow slanting eyes, high cheekbones and slender build. He said his childhood couldn't have been happier. He loved the journey to Kos, when for two months the family and their corgi made their way across

Europe in the Land-Rover, dragging behind them a caravan they slept in. 'It was funny, it was fabulous,' he said.

Stephen was the last of the family to see Ben.

'He said: "Bike, bike," and I said, "No chance, go to Granddad."' Then Stephen got on his bike and didn't look back.

Because of this, when he was questioned by the police he was singled out for attention. They said that his moped looked as if it had been involved in an accident. Stephen told them about a minor crash a few days before, when he'd swerved to avoid some tourists on quad bikes, which explained the lack of indicators and a smashed fairing. But they weren't satisfied. 'You fall off, kill the child, bury him?' the policeman said. The questioning had gone on like this over three or four days. 'They tried to break him,' was how Eddie had put it, 'but there was nothing to break.'

When the family returned from Kos, though, Stephen got back into a normal pace of life much sooner than his sister and parents did. Within two years he was living with a girlfriend and by the time he was twenty-three, he had two daughters. He was working on a building site, had passed his driving test and was enjoying life. But his relationship with the girls' mother started to break down, and eventually he left.

'I know nobody would understand someone walking away from their kids,' he said. 'It killed me. If I'd stayed I wouldn't have been able to carry on. I'd have given up. I was already going through emotional stress: it was either leave and get away from it or go down with the sinking ship. But I was bonded with my children and that's what nearly killed me.'

Ever since the police questioned Stephen, their idea that he might have had a hand in Ben's disappearance has haunted him. 'Did I take him, did I pick him up and put him on my bike, did I drive down that lane and take him away? I was questioning my own sanity. It was always there. How could a child disappear, how could he just vanish? Did I forget him somewhere or have an accident? Did I run over him or fall off my bike? I've asked myself that again and again.'

In 2001, when another television documentary was made to

coincide with the tenth anniversary of Ben's disappearance, Stephen was asked if he would be interviewed and whether he would undergo a form of hypnotherapy on camera. He says he agreed because he'd heard it might help to retrieve hidden memories. In the film he had to revisit the last moment he saw Ben and confront the doubt created by the police interrogation. It was traumatic, but when the filming was over, Stephen walked away sure that any suspicion that he or anyone else might have harboured that he could have accidentally killed Ben would be dispelled once and for all. Despite this, and although the film exonerates him, Stephen's fears were justified.

A year ago, he was out having a drink with his brother Danny and Kerry's husband, Craig. 'One of my mates was half-asleep drunk on a sofa and a group of lads were threatening him, so I went over and said, "Give up, he's drunk," and one of them went, "Oh, aren't you that uncle of that Ben that disappeared?" I said yes. "You took him on your bike, didn't you?"'

It's taken him years to understand how the trauma of Ben going missing has affected him. 'Our feelings were on hold when we were all trying to resolve Ben's case, so your own emotions get waylaid. And then when it starts to fade away, that's when you're left with yourself. If I hadn't have been through that experience in Greece, I'd have been mentally stronger and more able to deal with the problems, to work through things.' When I asked him how much he thought his adult life has been determined by losing Ben, he said, 'It's been destroyed, hasn't it, really?'

The one member of the Needham family who never knew Ben is Leighanna, his little sister. As a toddler she resembled Ben so much that they could have been twins. You look at her and you see Ben the baby; you look at her again and wonder if that is what Ben would look like now. It was this resemblance to Ben that led Kerry to agree, when Leighanna was twenty-one months old, that she should go with Christine and Eddie to Kos, to take part in a television reconstruction. Leighanna was the same age Ben was when he disappeared. Her hair, which was the same colour as Ben's, was cut short so she would look even more like him and the television crew filmed her in Herakles, walking out of the house and on to the lane, to see if it could offer any clues.

She was nearly fourteen when I met her last year, but her face still had a childlike quality. She said she remembered going to Kos, and when I asked whether it had felt like a sad experience, she said, 'Yep. It was funny though.

'There was a cameraman in front of me,' she said. 'I wouldn't go up the road so he told me to follow the duck. I had to follow a toy duck.' She went further and faster than they had ever imagined Ben could have done, which chilled her grandparents as they looked on.

Leighanna had started to ask questions about Ben when she was around five. 'She used to look through the photographs and say, "Who could be this?"' Kerry said. 'Those were her words, "Who could be this?"'

At primary school, her missing brother made her an object of special interest. Occasionally she was bullied. Other girls would say they knew where he was and once, when a hearse went by, a girl said for all she knew Ben could be in it. Leighanna, who says she is 'mouthy' like her mother, gave back as good as she got.

She feels protective of her mother. 'I've got to look after her. Mum'll think I don't love her if I don't fight for her or help her with things. I don't want her to get hurt more than she already is. Sometimes I can't tell her everything I want to – where it feels like Ben came first. Because there's been newspaper articles when my mum said she didn't know if she could love me as much as she loved Ben, because of what happened to him. I used to get really upset about it, even though I know Mum loves me as much as she loves Ben. I'd cry and it would make her cry. Sometimes the more we talk about things, the more upsetting it gets.'

When I saw them a few months later, Kerry told me Leighanna had talked to her more openly of her feelings about Ben. She said she thought Leighanna had agreed to be interviewed because there were things she wanted to say to her mother and couldn't. 'I think she knew she had to tell me things. I can't help her if I don't know.'

Leighanna tests the boundaries as any teenager would. But Kerry isn't any mother. She is acutely aware of her heightened sense of danger. 'You automatically presume everything's bad. But you can't let yourself think like that, because then she won't be safe when she goes out into the world on her own – because she's been protected too much. I knew I had to let her go.

'When she wasn't around it was like part of me was missing again and I couldn't settle. The hours she was out of the house I was pacing, looking at the phone – is someone going to phone me and say something's happened to her? I don't want to damage her, I have to let her go and find her own way, to become independent, her own person. She shouldn't be living in the shadow of my paranoia. She's already living in the shadow of Ben's disappearance.'

Leighanna says even though she's never met Ben, she feels like a sister to him. 'It's weird – you don't know where he is or even who he is. *He* probably doesn't know who he is.' She described a dream she'd had about him: 'I was running, running and running, and he seemed to be getting further away every time I ran towards him. He was running towards me and I was running towards him but it seemed like a never-ending run and every time I would try and grab him he was always a couple of steps in front, so I couldn't, and then I woke up and it was maddening. It was horrible.

'It's the first time I've ever had a dream like that although I've had loads of dreams before, waking up crying because I've dreamed we were in Kos and the police come to us and say they've found a body they think might be Ben's and we have to go and look at it and see if it is actually Ben's and then I look up just as we walk through to see if it is and I never find out.' ■

James Joyce as a child, 1888

A GHOST STORY

Rick Gekoski

I t's lost. All that is known of the poem are the following lines:

> His quaint-perched aerie on the crags of Time
> Where the rude din of this...century
> Can trouble him no more.

This fragment carries a special power for me, as if I last heard it in
the nursery. I seem, alas, to have set it on an internal loop to the tune
of 'Camptown Races', that catchy chronicle of running and gambling.
It drives me crazy when I can't make it stop. *Can trouble him no more!*
Trouble him no more! His quaint-perched aerie on the crags of Time Can
trouble him no more!

There's no sense trying to guess the author: these lines were
written when he was nine years old. Kids could write like this in the
nineteenth century, if they were bright and had the right schooling.
Oscar Wilde turned out reams of such stuff, and not only when he was
a child.

I am a dealer in rare books, and the blank spaces of this poem are an obsession of mine. I'm longing to know what opening it might have had, how it developed, and most of all what it looked like. But what I really want is to own it, this cheaply printed broadside. I'm haunted by the faint possibility of its discovery, by the unfinished business of that unpromising text. It is embarrassing, this greed, without scholarly or aesthetic dimension, in need, almost, of psychological explanation and treatment. *To be the only person who owns a copy.* To show it off, appear in the papers and on telly clutching it, reading its immature lines with as straight a face as possible. Howard Carter, returned from the young king's tomb, bearing lost treasure.

I n the opening chapter of James Joyce's *A Portrait of the Artist as a Young Man,* we overhear a violent family altercation at Christmas dinner, and though the book is a novel, I have little doubt that such an event actually took place in the Joyce household. The Irish nationalist Charles Stewart Parnell had died only a couple of months earlier, and Joyce's father was in a rage about the circumstances of his death.

In the following chapter, away at school at Clongowes, Stephen recalls the incident. 'He saw himself sitting at his table in Bray the morning after the discussion at the Christmas dinner table, trying to write a poem about Parnell... But his brain had then refused to grapple with the theme and, desisting, he had covered the page with the names and addresses of certain of his classmates...'

But the nine-year-old Joyce did, in life if not in fiction, compose the eulogistic verses that his younger brother Stanislaus referred to as 'the Parnell poem'. (Joyce later sanctioned the Latinate title 'Et Tu Healy', which may or may not be the original.) Stanislaus, to whose imperfect memory we owe the three surviving lines, described the poem as: 'a diatribe against the supposed traitor, Tim Healy, who had ratted at the bidding of the Catholic bishops and become a virulent enemy of Parnell, and so the piece was an echo of those political rancours that formed the theme of my father's nightly, half-drunken rantings...'

Stanislaus also reported that John Joyce, delighted by his son's production, had it printed, and distributed the broadsides to admirers

– 'I have a distinct recollection of my father's bringing home a roll of thirty or forty of them' – and that, in the (largely destroyed) thousand-page first draft of *A Portrait*, later published under the title *Stephen Hero*, 'my brother referred to the remaining broadsheets, of which the young Stephen Dedalus had been so proud, lying on the floor torn and muddied by the boots of the furniture removers,' when the family moved to Blackrock in 1892.

Both of these memories were later confirmed by John Joyce himself. When asked whether the broadsheet really existed, he responded: 'Remember it? Why shouldn't I remember it? Didn't I pay for the printing of it and didn't I send a copy to the Pope?' We catch the voice of a braggart here, too many 'I's' and not enough 'he's', the young author subsumed under his father's shallow egotism.

Repeated enquiries to the Vatican Library by bibliographic busybodies have not unearthed this copy of the poem. Presumably it was thrown out – can they really preserve every insignificant titbit that is sent in for the Pope's approval? – but it's a beguiling thought that it might be there, somewhere. Perhaps it has been misfiled and disregarded, like the Salisbury Cathedral copy of the Magna Carta, which disappeared for twenty years because it had been placed in the wrong drawer. 'Et Tu Healy' is not merely obscure, it is intrinsically uninteresting. There has been virtually nothing written about it. No sustained consideration, no single article, just a few passing mentions, most of them decades ago. There's just not enough material to work on, even in the avidly exegetical Joyce industry. Even in my years as a university teacher, when I occasionally taught courses on Joyce, I had no interest in 'Et Tu Healy', lost or found. What did it matter? As a rare-book dealer, however, my non-interest has morphed into an obsession.

I don't know how I became a dealer. It snuck up on me. I began collecting as a boy in Washington DC, laying down a lifetime pattern of wanting and hunting, of desire, frustration and occasional satisfaction.

When I was seven, Topps (a company previously best known for making Bazooka Bubblegum) began issuing baseball cards, and I, like all of my friends, was immediately obsessed by them. For a nickel you got five cards and a flat piece of gum that was unchewably stiff, nastily over-sugared and invariably thrown away. The ideal was to acquire all of the twenty-five players on your team – mine was the Washington Senators, though I switched allegiance to the Brooklyn Dodgers when we moved to Long Island in 1954. Topps knew how to get you hooked: most of the cards were common, but the most desirable ones were issued in much smaller quantities. We boys would buy and buy, yearning to fill our gaps. At Topps there must have been an avalanche of nickels rolling in.

I was desperate to get the card for the Senators' first baseman Mickey Vernon, my favourite player, who led the American League in batting in 1953. I bought and bought, leafed avidly through the five cards. Wrong teams! Wrong players! No Mickey. I had to have him and I offered remarkable enticements to a friend who did – mountains of my duplicates, or a choice of the scarce cards I knew he needed. Knowing how much I yearned for my hero – in acquiring the card you magically acquired the person – he declined, reckoning he'd get a better deal in the future. I cajoled, pleaded, ranted. No dice.

To outflank my mean (soon to be ex-) friend, I went to the shop that sold used comics and baseball cards, where the choices were as wide as the prices were intimidating. The dealer was a podgy red-faced old man (most men were old) in a soiled Yankees shirt, with lank grey hair and a bored expression. (I don't know if he had acne, but memory requires it, so I have given him some.) On those interminable hot summer days my father would watch benignly as I prowled about in the stifling gloom.

Dad didn't collect anything himself – he had a large number of books that were casually acquired rather than compulsively assembled – but he was amused by my ardour, and when we got back to my grandparents' bungalow, where we spent the summers, he would take a few minutes with me as I installed my acquisitions into my collection. I shocked Granny Pearl by spending five dollars on a card that I'd been wanting for ages. I kept it on my bedside table for a week, and showed it off to envious friends, before putting it in the White Owl cigar box that Poppa Norman had given me, and forgetting about it. I was offered one or two tempting trades, but declined to part with my treasure except in a swap for a Mickey. No deal. I regularly and intemperately accused Topps of unfair practice: manipulation of the market meant manipulation of me. Scarcity engenders need.

In most boys the collecting mania fades after adolescence. My stamp collections and Lionel trains went on to my closet shelf, from which they eventually but mysteriously disappeared; my Topps cards in their cigar box, too, obscurely decamped. I never regretted the loss of the stamps and trains, but the early Topps became highly collectable in later years (a 1952 Mickey Mantle rookie card is worth $75,000 today), and I must have had a few that would have become valuable. And that, of course, is *why* they become desirable, as boy collector after boy collector shelved them, and myriad moms threw them out in a clear-up as the erstwhile fanatic went to college and entered that collecting latency period from which few emerge. If you return to collecting as an adult, it is more often art or furniture, carpets or ceramics perhaps. Or books, though not many go that route. There are very few book collectors, and almost no one understands them. We hardly understand ourselves.

My unappetizing acquaintance with the baseball-card dealer hardly served as a role model for rare-book dealing – no one entering that dusty room could have thought, 'I want to be like him, that's just the job for me!' I wanted my Mickey Vernon card because what I most dreamed of was to *be* Mickey Vernon. I played first base at school and later in Little League: first baseman was a life plan, dealer was not.

You couldn't, until quite recently, train as a book dealer, and though there are now MA courses in the subject I don't entirely believe in them. You learn the trade willy-nilly, by trial and (mostly) error. You pay for your mistakes, buying the wrong thing, or the right one at the wrong price. You learn quickly. During my time writing my DPhil at Oxford, I haunted the local used bookshops, and it became a challenge

to see if I could pay for my holidays by scouting – Americans call it
'running' – and selling my purchases at a profit to members of the
book trade. On visits home, my father became fascinated by my new
vocation, and would sit in his Eames chair, put his record of *The Magic
Flute* on his new Danish teak hi-fi, and quiz me on values. The guide
in those days was Van Allen Bradley's *The Book Collector's Handbook
of Values.*

'*Brighton Rock?*' he'd ask.

'One of the scarcer ones, especially in dust wrapper. Bradley's
wrong on it, I'll bet.'

'He says $100–$200.'

'I'd pay $500 if I could find one and if you'd lend me the money.'

He would have. He was uncommonly engaged with my new
incarnation, possibly because it was the first time I had deviated from
the directions he'd laid down. I'd majored in English at the University
of Pennsylvania, as he had, and, after outgrowing my desire to be a
baseball player, wanted first to become a psychoanalyst, if not that a
university English teacher and, failing that, a lawyer. He'd wanted the
same things in the same order, and though mildly satisfied to have
ended up in law, he was glad I hadn't done so myself. Lecturing was
better, and this book running better yet. No one in the family had ever
been good at business, and my combination of literary and financial
acumen fascinated him. I would come home from New York after a
day's scouting, with a few hundred dollars profit in my pocket, and we
would both be lost in admiration. We contemplated setting up a
business together: Son and Gekoski, Rare Books.

He died in 1980, at the age of sixty-eight. Though the cause was
pancreatic cancer, in some ways I think he just wore out. As he lay
peacefully awaiting the end, he said, 'I never had much energy,' as if
that explained it. Though he outlived my mother by eleven years, and
she had bags of it (most of it misdirected), my father wasn't built to
last, and seemed not to regret it. I did, terribly. His virtues were
Chaucerian: largeness of vision, freedom from cant, shrewdness,
benignity. He treated everyone he met with the same quiet respect,

lived an exemplary inner life, and would have died reconciled to his God if he'd had one. His example and legacy became part of my psychological and moral cellular structure and his death, like his life, formed and enabled me. His financial legacy – I inherited £60,000 from him in 1981 – allowed me to pursue my passion, and I added gem after gem to my collection of rare books and manuscripts: the corrected typescript of Virginia Woolf's *Freshwater*, the only known copy of *Sons and Lovers* in a dust wrapper, a pre-publication inscribed copy of *Almayer's Folly* (Conrad's first novel), and best of all, a fine first edition of *Ulysses*.

The example of, and yearning for, Mickey Vernon's baseball card provided the source and template for these manic acquisitions: my collecting was driven by love, scarcity and psychic identification. In acquiring a baseball card, you alchemically incorporated the actual player; so too owning first editions by Eliot and Joyce brought me closer to them, made them mine, made them me. I wanted the best things – the best writers – that Dad's money could buy, regretting only that he was not there to watch approvingly as my cigar box filled.

A year later I issued my first catalogue, *R.A. Gekoski Modern First Editions*, and sold my whole collection. I had found to my surprise that the pleasure of ownership diminished sharply over time. Once a card went into the box it seldom came out again. From gloating over my *Ulysses* to taking it for granted took only a few months. Anyway, Dad's money having run out, the only way to insure fresh examples of the precious and rare was to sell what I had. In my new life as a dealer the initial emotional structure applied: to buy, and to sell, only what is the cause of pride and delight, to acquire what is rare and well-nigh unobtainable, to specialize in the Mickey Vernon cards of the rare-book trade.

Analogies with drug addiction are inescapable: you end up dealing in order to support your habit. Being a dealer has a further advantage: not only do I buy the best things that I can locate and afford, I get to display them to a constituency that understands what I am doing. If collecting is isolated and atomistic, dealing is a form of self-display:

here, my first catalogue proclaimed, is the result of connoisseurship, here is what I can do, what I am.

This partly explains, I suppose, my fascination with 'Et Tu Healy': what could be more desirable than offering this apparently unobtainable ghost by one of my revered authors? Yet even this doesn't explain, quite, the intensity of my desire to locate a copy. Generally I fixate on material that is rare, expensive and important, but it would be hard to claim much in the way of scholarly or even biographical significance for this scrap of a poem.

No, its magnetism has something to do with my father. 'Et Tu Healy' was written by James Joyce when he was nine, in response to imperatives that were surely derivative: the little boy expressing what his father felt. The poem, psychologically, is an unconscious act of identification and homage from son to father. Perhaps that is why I find the story of it – the text of the poem itself doesn't matter – so moving, why it unconsciously recalls my attachment to my own father, my childish wish to talk and to be like him.

'Et Tu Healy' is not a ghost (a book for which the publication has been announced, but is never produced) in the strict bibliographic sense, but it's close enough for me. How can you tell, quite, if a book has been announced and never printed, or announced, printed, and then lost?

Given that Joyce's bibliographers, Slocum and Cahoon, are the first point of call for queries of this kind, it is disappointing how wrong they are about 'Et Tu Healy', of which they cite seven lines, the three with which I began, plus the following four:

> My cot alas that dear old shady home
> Where oft in youthful sport I played
> Upon thy verdant grassy fields all day
> Or lingered for a moment in thy bosom shade.

The cited authority for this attribution is Stanislaus Joyce's *Recollections of James Joyce*, but reference to that text makes it clear that he was *distinguishing* these unprepossessing lines from those of 'the Parnell poem', not including them in it. In a letter to Harriet Shaw Weaver in November of 1930, Joyce himself cited this quatrain, which he said he was going to use in *Finnegans Wake* in a game of Angels and Devils (here represented by Shaun), who 'maunders off into sentimental poetry of what I actually wrote at the age of nine.' There is something touchingly appropriate in the clumsiness of the phrase, from which a word or two seem to have been omitted. The game, and the poem, Joyce told Miss Weaver, were soon 'interrupted by a violent pang of toothache after which he [Shaun] throws a fit,' which may represent an act of literary self-criticism.

I do not believe that Joyce's category 'sentimental poetry' would have included 'Et Tu Healy', which is written in an altogether different register than 'My Cot, Alas', so we must reduce what we know of that text by more than half: our ghost is getting ghostlier.

After three decades during which almost no significant Joyce manuscript material emerged, all of a sudden there is such a quantity of it – letters, inscribed books, working notebooks, whole chapters of *Ulysses*, draft material for *Finnegans Wake* – that one wonders if an assiduous forger has secreted himself in a Martello tower to produce it. A lag between an author's death and the arrival on the market of important letters, inscribed books and manuscripts is not unusual. The mother lode – material held by the author himself, his closest friends and family – often takes decades to emerge, having been passed down the generations until someone decides that the choice between some old letters or manuscripts and a retreat in Provence is a no-brainer. Recent sales of such Joyce material have realized prices sufficient to throw in a modest yacht as well.

In the last six years the National Library of Ireland, which previously lacked any significant Joyce manuscripts, has spent over £10 million on manuscript material for both *Ulysses* and *Finnegans Wake*. Descendants of Stanislaus Joyce, John Quinn (the New York lawyer and collector who purchased a manuscript version of *Ulysses* from Joyce in the 1920s) and Joyce's friend and amanuensis Paul Leon have all sold material that alters our understanding of Joyce's achievement. In addition, manuscripts emerging from a Paris bookseller have thrown new light on the history of the composition of both *Ulysses* and *Finnegans Wake*, and I am told that T. S. Eliot's library – which has been visited by only a handful of scholars – contains fourteen previously unrecorded letters from Joyce to Eliot.

There is a gravitational pull when new discoveries are announced and rewarded: it makes people search their attics a little more thoroughly and reconsider whether it might just be the right time to sell. Could the present glut of Joyce material, and its attendant publicity, unearth that elusive copy of 'Et Tu Healy'? What if it showed up in some disregarded bureau, or interleaved in an old atlas or directory? If there is one – *surely* there is one – it must be in Dublin somewhere.

In my world when you're talking ghosts you're talking money. But who'd buy it? I can think of a couple of private collectors, but until confronted with a copy, one couldn't really say. Books, like pictures, are valued by both hand and eye: they need to have some kind of visceral appeal, some crackle and pop, which Jeanette Winterson nicely calls their 'psychometry'. Perhaps the mystique might evaporate when an actual copy emerges and is seen for the trifle that it really is.

But let's suppose one was found. There would be a fuss, as the proud new owner showed off his or her treasure, though by a neat irony the text could not be printed in its entirety due to the assiduous protectiveness of the Joyce estate. The old eagle in his aerie overlooking the world is not, in this instance, the ghost of the late Parnell, but Steven James Joyce, the author's grandson, and guardian of all things Joycean. So protectively litigious is he that even Sotheby's, when they illustrate a Joyce manuscript, have been required to blur the image discreetly, as if it were a model's pubic hair in an old-fashioned nudie picture.

Word would get out, and I would find a way to see and read it, the result of which, surely, would be the diminishing of my interest in the poem, a stripping of its black tulip numinosity – the banishment of my ghost. Bookselling fetishizes objects, but usually they are more or less worth the fuss. But 'Et Tu Healy'? Fetishization one hundred, object zero. This fact, for surely it is that, locates something that lurks disturbingly at the heart of my way of life, for when you are in search of treasure – surely the animating archetype of collecting and dealing – you have to enter the caves, push aside the bears, root about among the bones. There is excitement here, but also something psychically dangerous, which, on its occasional outbreaks, produces a sense of futility so intense that I find it incapacitating.

Ambrose Bierce's *Devil's Dictionary* defines a ghost as the outward manifestation of an inner fear. This is fair enough: we are frightened of death, and those spooks in sheets are the objective correlative of our terror. As they hover in the night, *hoo*-ing and *woo*-ing, we are reminded of the evanescence of human life, its short span, the long emptiness to come. 'Et Tu Healy' plays a similar role in my life, and is similarly charged: the rattling of its baby chains engenders a spasm of anxiety in me, as if my book-dealing life has been dedicated to futile pursuits and meaningless goals. Has there been something unworthy about it, snuffling about for trifles?

Perhaps if 'Et Tu Healy' rejoined the world, I might look it in the eye, make an adjustment in our long relations, and rid myself of my embarrassing obsession. What would we be left with? Just a rare piece of paper, a poem written by a little boy and published by his proud father, transformed too quickly from a touching memento to a scrap under the removal men's boots. Lovely thing in its way, with its loss built into its very nature, and once found thoroughly forgettable. Just the only known copy of 'Et Tu Healy' – nothing haunting about that. Perhaps then that quaint aerie perched on the crags of time *would* trouble me no more, though if that were to happen I would, curiously, rather regret it.

Being haunted by a lost scrap and occasionally tormented by a repetitive inner melody is a small price to pay for the delight of the chase, however futile. That excitement is strong enough to resist its shadow, and the continued loss of 'Et Tu Healy' suits me just fine. The delicate tendrils that attach 'Et Tu Healy', my father and me require a subterranean ground to thrive, and are nourished in the poem's absence. It can be a bad mistake, if you are a collector, making the unconscious conscious; if a copy were located, something of him, and me – and of us together – would be endangered.

I hope it never gets found. ∎

CONTRIBUTORS

Elena Baglioni is completing her doctorate in Development Studies at the University of Bologna. She has researched poverty-reduction strategies, agrarian change and land access in Senegal.

John Burnside has published six works of fiction and eleven collections of poetry, including *The Asylum Dance*, which won the 2000 Whitbread Poetry Award. A new collection of poems, *The Hunt in the Forest*, will appear in August. He last featured in *Granta* 96 with 'The Limeroom'.

Bruce Connew is a social and political documentary photographer, based in New Zealand and Paris.

Janet Frame (1924–2004) was a novelist, poet, essayist and short-story writer. Her autobiography inspired Jane Campion's acclaimed film, *An Angel at My Table*. She was an honorary foreign member of the American Academy of Arts and Letters and in 1983 she was awarded a CBE.

Georgia Garrett is a literary agent at AP Watt Ltd.

Rick Gekoski is the author of *Tolkien's Gown and Other Stories of Great Authors and Rare Books*. His second series of *Lost, Stolen or Shredded: The History of Some Missing Works of Art* will air on BBC Radio 4 later this year and *Outside of a Dog: A Bibliomemoir* will be published in the autumn.

A.L. Kennedy is the author of five novels, two books of non-fiction and four collections of short stories. 'Story of My Life' will be published in *What Becomes* in August 2009. Her last novel, *Day*, won the Costa Prize in 2008 and she has twice been named one of *Granta*'s Best of Young British Novelists. She last appeared in the magazine with 'God and Me', published in *Granta* 93.

Andrew Martin is writing a series of detective novels set on the railways in the early twentieth century. The latest, *The Last Train to Scarborough*, has just been published.

Melanie McFadyean is a freelance journalist. She lives in London and teaches part-time at City University's journalism department. 'Five Houses' featured in *Granta* 95.

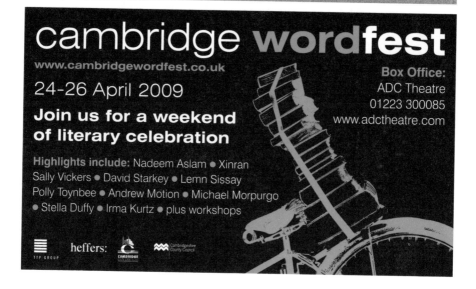

Mimi Mollica has covered assignments around the world for a number of magazines and NGOs. His photo essays have won several awards and have been widely exhibited. Most recently he won the European Parliament photo competition, 'Resolution '09'.

Jan Morris explored dreaming, memory and the art of embarrassment in *Granta* 87 with 'Perchance to Pick One's Nose'. She is the Anglo-Welsh author of some forty books of travel, autobiography, history and fiction. She is eighty-two years old and lives in the village of Llanystumdwy, Gwynedd.

Don Paterson is a poet, editor and musician and teaches at the University of St Andrews. His poem 'The Swing' appeared in *Granta* 100 and a new collection, *Two Trees*, will be published this September.

Elizabeth Pisani was a foreign correspondent and reported, between 1986 and 1995, from India, China, Indonesia, Vietnam, Cambodia and elsewhere, mostly for Reuters. *The Wisdom of Whores: Bureaucrats, Brothels and the Business of Aids* was published in 2008.

Craig Taylor is the editor of the online magazine *Five Dials* and the author of *One Million Tiny Plays About Britain* and *Return to Akenfield*, part of which was included in *Granta* 90.

Jeremy Treglown's *V.S. Pritchett: A Working Life* (2005) was shortlisted for the Whitbread Award for Biography and the Duff Cooper Prize. His piece 'Closing Time' appeared in *Granta* 94.

Altán Walker (1964–2007) was born in Northern Ireland. She trained as a lawyer and worked in television before becoming a full-time writer.

Maurice Walsh grew up in County Tipperary and has lived in Managua, Santiago and Mexico City. *The News from Ireland: Foreign Correspondents and the Irish Revolution* came out in October 2008.

Contributing Editors

Diana Athill, Jonathan Derbyshire, Sophie Harrison, Isabel Hilton, Blake Morrison, Philip Oltermann, John Ryle, Sukhdev Sandhu, Lucretia Stewart.

GRANTA | 106

ANNIVERSARY FICTION ISSUE

To celebrate its thirtieth birthday, *Granta* brings you an extra issue this summer. Dedicated to the most exciting and vibrant new fiction from around the world, the issue is filled with wonderful short stories, extracts from works-in-progress and a thought-provoking survey of the contemporary literary landscape. Plus: **Jhumpa Lahiri**, author of the highly acclaimed collection *Unaccustomed Earth*, travels to Paris to interview one of the world's most accomplished short-story writers, **Mavis Gallant**.

www.granta.com

Subscribers to *Granta* enjoy the full benefits of our Website, including access to our archive and membership to our online community. Granta.com offers insight, opinion, fiction, blogs, news and special offers – and it's all free and updated daily. You can find out more about *Granta* 106 on granta.com, including interviews with our contributors and short films.

Web exclusives: **Michael Peel** investigates the dirty business of oil, from a US warship in the Gulf of Guinea; **Paul Currion** reports from Iraqi Kurdistan; and read letters from the *Granta* archive by **Kazuo Ishiguro** and **Martha Gellhorn**. Visit granta.com to join in the discussion.